FOUNDING OF T
THIRTE
COLONIES

READING COMPREHENSION

TRUE OR FALSE

After reading about the **New England Colonies**, read each statement below and determine if it is true or false. If the statement is true, color the coin that corresponds with that question. If the statement is false, cross out that coin value. When you are finished, add the TOTAL of **ALL TRUE** coin values to reveal a 4-digit code. One digit of the code has been provided for you. If the total is 625, a 6 would go in the first box, the 2 in the second box and so on.

A 75 | B 25 | C 50 | D 100 | E 100 | F 75 | G 50 | H 25

A. The English often imposed their laws and practices on the Native Americans.

B. In the 1600s, England was experiencing religious turmoil (chaos).

C. As the governor of Plymouth, John Mason helped the Pilgrims survive their early years in New England.

D. The New England Colonies included Maine, Pennsylvania, Ohio, and Connecticut.

E. Rhode Island was founded by William Bradford.

F. Religion was the cornerstone of life in the New England Colonies.

G. The Pilgrims sought to separate entirely from the Church of England.

H. Rhode Island became a place for Puritans and Quakers to express religious beliefs publicly.

After shading the coins based on your answer, add the value of ALL TRUE statements to get the final total. Record your answer in the boxes below.

7

MYSTERY WORD

After reading about the **Middle Colonies**, determine if each statement below is true or false. Color or shade the boxes of the **TRUE** statements. Next, unscramble the mystery word using the large letters of the **TRUE** statements.

Delaware was founded by Peter Minuit. **R**	Carpenters built homes, barns, bridges, and other infrastructures necessary for daily life. **E**	The first permanent European settlement in Delaware was named Fort Christina. **C**	The counties in Delaware established their own assembly in 1704. **L**
Delaware's rivers provided routes for transporting goods to larger hubs. **T**	In 1609, Francis Drake navigated up the Hudson River to Albany, New York. **S**	In 1681, William Penn, a Quaker, received a land grant from King Charles II. **U**	Queen Anne reunited East and West Jersey in 1702. **I**
Edward Hyde was appointed the first governor of the royal colony of Vermont. **D**	Middle Colonies included New York, Pennsylvania, New Jersey and Delaware. **R**	New York was originally settled by the German. **P**	Traditionally, blacksmiths worked with iron and steel. **U**
King Charles II granted the land to his brother, the Duke of York. **A**	William Penn's charter guaranteed freedom of religion. **G**	Delaware later came under English control in 1687. **B**	The poor soil in the Middle Colonies only supported a small range of crops. **O**

Unscramble the word using the large bold letters of only the **TRUE** statements.

MULTIPLE CHOICE

After reading about **New Hampshire**, answer each multiple-choice question below. Then, count the number of times you used each letter as an answer (ABCD) to reveal a 4-digit code. Letters may be used more than once or not at all. If a letter option is not used, put a zero in that box.

1. What did the economy of New Hampshire rely on?
   A. Fishing
   B. Timber
   C. Agriculture
   D. All of the above
2. What did the extensive forests of New Hampshire provide wood for?
   A. Construction
   B. Fuel
   C. Shipbuilding
   D. All of the above
3. In the 1600s, when Europeans arrived, who was the New Hampshire region home to?
   A. Abenaki
   B. Pennacook
   C. Algonquian
   D. All of the above
4. Mason was the former governor of what region?
   A. Providence
   B. Exeter
   C. Newfoundland
   D. Jamestown
5. Mason and Gorges split the land based on what river?
   A. Punxatawny River
   B. Piscataqua River
   C. Potomac River
   D. None of the above
6. What religious groups settled in New Hampshire?
   A. Quakers
   B. Anglicans
   C. Puritans
   D. All of the above
7. When was Captain Mason granted a royal charter by King James I?
   A. 1609
   B. 1619
   C. 1629
   D. 1639
8. Who founded Exeter, New Hampshire?
   A. Wheelwright
   B. Gorges
   C. Jones
   D. Williams

Count how many times you used each letter as a correct answer (ABCD) to determine the 4-digit code. Record your answer in the boxes below.

# of A's | # of B's | # of C's | # of D's

MYSTERY MATCH

After reading about the **Salem Witch Trials**, draw a line from the left-hand column to make a match in the right-hand column. Your line should go through **ONE** letter. When you complete all the matches, use the letters with a line THROUGH them to unscramble a mystery word. You MUST start and end your line at the **arrow points**.

Cotton Mather	Length of the Salem Witch Trials
Six months	Argued for due process of law
William Griggs	Dreams and visions
Puritans	First person executed in Salem
William Phips	Doctor who diagnosed the afflicted
Spectral Evidence	Governor of Salem
Tituba	Strict Christians
Bridget Bishop	Confessed under pressure

A E B F H M I P R R K S T Y S H

Unscramble the 8 letters to reveal a mystery word:

DOUBLE PUZZLE

After reading about **North Carolina**, determine the word that corresponds with the statements provided below. Spell the corresponding word in the boxes to the right. You may or may not use all squares provided for each answer. Any numerical answers must be spelled out. Next, use the numbers **under** indicated letters to reveal a secret word.

1. First permanent town established in North Carolina
2. Last name of the proprietor that refused to sell his one-eighth share
3. The Tuscarora migrated northward to join the ___ Confederacy
4. The ___ Church became the official church in the 1700s
5. Quakers mostly settled in the ___ region
6. Synonym for proprietors
7. Number of proprietors that King Charles I granted charters to
8. Carolina comes from the Latin word "___"
9. Last name of English explorer that attempted to establish Roanoke
10. The Catawba were wiped out by a ___ epidemic

SECRET WORD 1 2 3 4 5 6 7 8 9

PARAGRAPH CODE

After reading about **Roanoke**, head back to the reading and number ALL the paragraphs in the reading passage. Then, read each statement below and determine which paragraph **NUMBER** the statement can be found in. Paragraph numbers MAY be used more than one time or not at all. Follow the directions below to reveal the 4-digit code.

A. The disappearance of the Roanoke settlers has sparked numerous theories over the centuries.

B. The expedition arrived at Roanoke about one year after Amada and Barlowe looked for places to settle a colony.

C. Due to the Spanish Armada, White was not able to return to Roanoke for three years.

D. The story of the Lost Colony of Roanoke is one of the oldest mysteries in American history.

E. The site of the original Roanoke settlement is now part of the Fort Raleigh National Historic Site.

F. There were ninety men, thirteen women, and eleven children.

G. England wanted to establish a colony as an attempt to expand the British Empire in the New World.

H. Raleigh sent Captain Amada and Captain Barlowe to explore the new area.

ELIMINATE ALL EVEN-NUMBERED paragraphs that you used as an answer. Record the remaining numbers (in the SAME order in which you recorded them above) in the boxes below.

SECRET CODES & MYSTERY WORDS

By Lisa Fink

Contact the author :
Lisa@ThinkTankTeacher.com

ABOUT THIS WORKBOOK

History doesn't have to be boring — especially when it comes with a dash of mystery and a twist of F-U-N, including secret codes and mystery words! This collection of **21** reading comprehension passages is designed to spark curiosity and make homeschool history curriculum come alive for kids ages 10+.

WHAT'S INSIDE?

21 Reading Passages: (2 full pages each)
Each passage is crafted to draw your kids into the past, making history relatable and intriguing for learners at home or in the classroom. To ensure understanding, each reading comprehension passage comes with two interactive worksheets.

Worksheet 1: Crack the 4-Digit Code!
This activity turns reading into a puzzle, keeping kids motivated to dive deeper into the material. Your learners will answer comprehension questions based on the passage and correct answers will reveal a secret 4-digit code. Programmable locks aren't required, but they can take the fun to the next level!

Worksheet 2: Mystery Word!
To ensure they've truly grasped the material, kids answer another set of questions, based on the same reading passage, that unveil a secret word.

WHY IT WORKS:

Active Engagement: By turning reading comprehension into a game, kids are more likely to stay engaged, motivated to learn and eager to finish the task. Game-based learning requires active participation. Rather than passively reading and answering questions, kids are actively seeking answers to solve the puzzle.

Encourages Critical Thinking: Game elements often require kids to think critically and make connections between different pieces of information. To find the correct answers and solve the puzzle, they must analyze the text carefully, improving their comprehension skills.

Reinforcement Through Fun: The excitement of uncovering codes and secret words reinforces key historical concepts in a way that sticks. Kids may be more willing to go back and re-read sections of the passage to ensure they have the correct answers.

Incentive to Learn: The reward of discovering a secret code or mystery word acts as a powerful incentive. Kids are more likely to pay close attention to details in the reading passage, knowing that each answer brings them closer to solving the puzzle. This can lead to a deeper understanding of the content.

Increased Motivation: When an assignment includes elements like secret codes or mystery words, it feels less like work and more like a fun challenge. This added layer of excitement motivates kids to complete the task to "win" or uncover the hidden element.

Versatile Use: These activities are perfect for homeschooling or classrooms — use as part of your daily lessons, supplemental homework, or independent study.

Promotes Positive Reinforcement: Successfully uncovering a secret code or mystery word provides immediate positive feedback, which reinforces the learning experience. This sense of achievement boosts confidence and encourages kids to tackle future activities with enthusiasm.

HOW TO FIND THE MYSTERY WORD

There are three different types of mystery word activities.

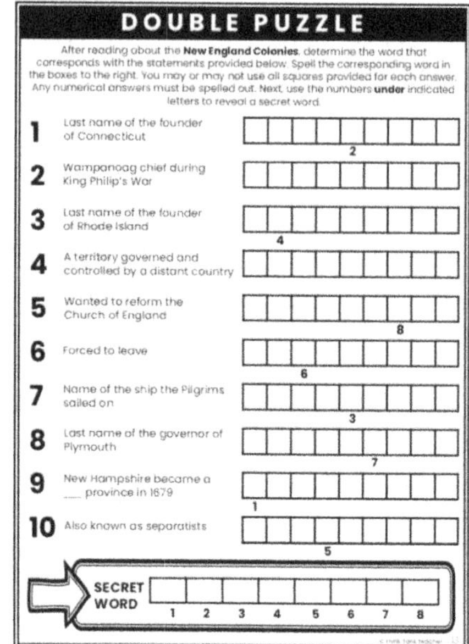

DOUBLE PUZZLE

After reading about the **New England Colonies**, determine the word that corresponds with the statements provided below. Spell the corresponding word in the boxes to the right. You may or may not use all squares provided for each answer. Any numerical answers must be spelled out. Next, use the numbers **under** indicated letters to reveal a secret word.

1 Last name of the founder of Connecticut

2 Wampanoag chief during King Philip's War

3 Last name of the founder of Rhode Island

4 A territory governed and controlled by a distant country

5 Wanted to reform the Church of England

6 Forced to leave

7 Name of the ship the Pilgrims sailed on

8 Last name of the governor of Plymouth

9 New Hampshire became a ___ province in 1679

10 Also known as separatists

SECRET WORD 1 2 3 4 5 6 7 8

DOUBLE PUZZLE

After reading the passage, determine the correct word that corresponds with statements 1-10. Spell the corresponding word in the boxes to the right. You may or may not use all squares provided for each answer. Any numerical answers **must** be spelled out. Next, use the numbers **under** indicated letters to reveal a secret word.

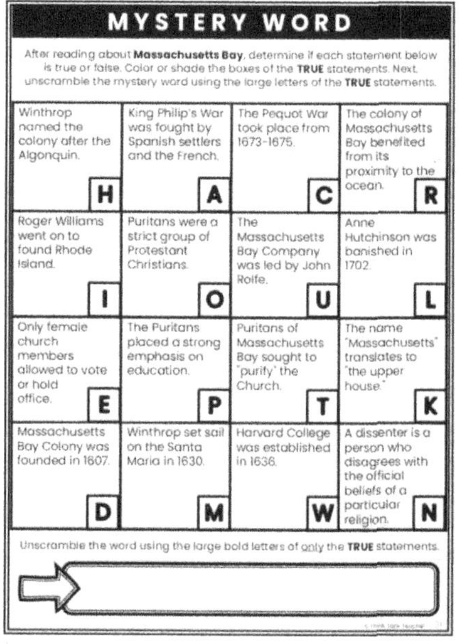

MYSTERY WORD

After reading about **Massachusetts Bay**, determine if each statement below is true or false. Color or shade the boxes of the **TRUE** statements. Next, unscramble the mystery word using the large letters of the **TRUE** statements.

Winthrop named the colony after the Algonquin. **H**	King Philip's War was fought by Spanish settlers and the French. **A**	The Pequot War took place from 1673-1675. **C**	The colony of Massachusetts Bay benefited from its proximity to the ocean. **R**
Roger Williams went on to found Rhode Island. **I**	Puritans were a strict group of Protestant Christians. **O**	The Massachusetts Bay Company was led by John Rolfe. **U**	Anne Hutchinson was banished in 1702. **L**
Only female church members allowed to vote or hold office. **E**	The Puritans placed a strong emphasis on education. **P**	Puritans of Massachusetts Bay sought to "purify" the Church. **T**	The name "Massachusetts" translates to "the upper house." **K**
Massachusetts Bay Colony was founded in 1607. **D**	Winthrop set sail on the Santa Maria in 1630. **M**	Harvard College was established in 1636. **W**	A dissenter is a person who disagrees with the official beliefs of a particular religion. **N**

Unscramble the word using the large bold letters of only the **TRUE** statements.

MYSTERY WORD

After reading the passage, determine if each statement is true or false. Color or shade the boxes of the **TRUE** statements. After all TRUE answers have been shaded, unscramble the mystery word using the large, bold letters of only the TRUE statements.

MYSTERY MATCH

After reading about **New Hampshire**, draw a line from the left-hand column to make a match in the right-hand column. Your line should go through **ONE** letter. When you complete all the matches, use the letters with a line THROUGH them to unscramble a mystery word. You MUST start and end your line at the **arrow points**.

Commodity	Year New Hampshire became a royal colony
Encroach	Unlawful intrusion into someone else's territory
Ferdinando Gorges	Year Exeter was founded
1679	Founder of Maine
Denomination	Products or goods
1638	Distinct religious group
King James I	Chosen for a job
Appoint	Granted royal charter to John Mason

L B A I N J D H H S T F P R D

Unscramble the 8 letters to reveal a mystery word:

MYSTERY MATCH

After reading the passage, draw a line from the left-hand column to make a match in the right-hand column. Your line should go THROUGH **one** letter. When you complete all the matches, use the letters with a line THROUGH them to unscramble a mystery word. You MUST start and end your line at the arrow points. Then, unscramble the 8 letters to reveal the mystery word. **IMPORTANT: Your line MUST start with an arrow TIP on the left and end at an arrow TIP on the right.** If you do not draw from arrow tip to arrow tip, you will not be able to reveal the hidden word.

HOW TO FIND THE SECRET CODE

There are three different types of secret code activities.

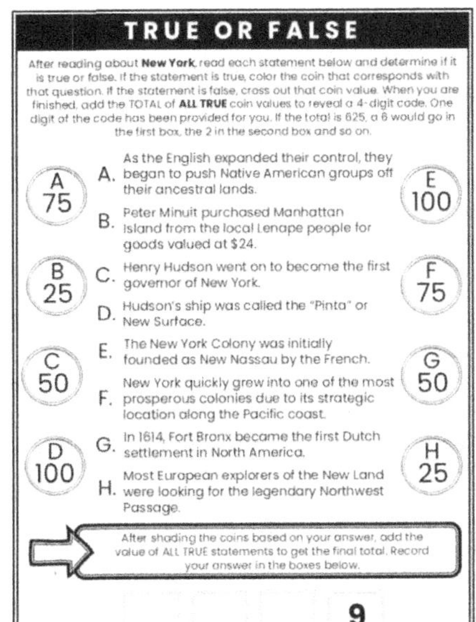

TRUE OR FALSE

After reading about **New York**, read each statement below and determine if it is true or false. If the statement is true, color the coin that corresponds with that question. If the statement is false, cross out that coin value. When you are finished, add the TOTAL of **ALL TRUE** coin values to reveal a 4-digit code. One digit of the code has been provided for you. If the total is 625, a 6 would go in the first box, the 2 in the second box and so on.

A 75 | B 25 | C 50 | D 100 | E 100 | F 75 | G 50 | H 25

A. As the English expanded their control, they began to push Native American groups off their ancestral lands.

B. Peter Minuit purchased Manhattan Island from the local Lenape people for goods valued at $24.

C. Henry Hudson went on to become the first governor of New York.

D. Hudson's ship was called the "Pinta" or New Surface.

E. The New York Colony was initially founded as New Nassau by the French.

F. New York quickly grew into one of the most prosperous colonies due to its strategic location along the Pacific coast.

G. In 1614, Fort Bronx became the first Dutch settlement in North America.

H. Most European explorers of the New Land were looking for the legendary Northwest Passage.

After shading the coins based on your answer, add the value of ALL TRUE statements to get the final total. Record your answer in the boxes below.

9

TRUE OR FALSE

After reading the passage, determine if each statement is true or false. If the statement is true, color, circle, or shade-in the coin that corresponds with that question. If the statement is false, cross out that coin value. When you are finished, add the **TOTAL** of **ALL TRUE** coin values to reveal a 4-digit code. If you are working on statement D, be sure you find the coin that is labeled D. The final number of the code will always be provided for you.

PARAGRAPH CODE

After reading about **Virginia**, head back to the reading and number ALL the paragraphs in the reading passage. Then, read each statement below and determine which paragraph **NUMBER** the statement can be found in. Paragraph numbers MAY be used more than one time or not at all. Follow the directions below to reveal the 4-digit code.

A The House of Burgesses was made up of twenty-two burgesses, or representatives.

B In 1612, John Rolfe successfully cultivated a strain of tobacco that was highly popular in England.

C This body allowed male property owners to elect representatives who would help make decisions for the colony.

D The Virginia Colony was the first permanent English settlement in North America.

E The church played a significant role in the colony's social and political life, with Anglican ministers often serving as community leaders.

F The company sent three ships - Susan Constant, Godspeed, and Discovery - to the New World, arriving near Chesapeake Bay.

G Subsistence farming is when farmers grow crops and raise livestock mainly to feed themselves and their families.

H The economy of the Virginia Colony was initially based on subsistence farming, fishing, and trading with Native Americans.

ELIMINATE ALL EVEN-NUMBERED paragraphs that you used as an answer. Record the remaining numbers (in the SAME order in which you recorded them above) in the boxes below.

PARAGRAPH CODE

After reading the passage, number **ALL** the paragraphs. Then, read each statement and determine which paragraph **NUMBER** the statement can be found in. Paragraph numbers MAY be used more than one time or not at all. When all paragraph numbers have been found, **ELIMINATE ALL EVEN-NUMBERED** paragraphs that you used as an answer. Record the remaining numbers (in the SAME order in which you recorded them) in the boxes at the bottom. **Example: 85362147 = 5317 (after crossing off all EVEN numbers, the remaining numbers in the order in which they were found is 5317)**

MULTIPLE CHOICE

After reading about **Georgia**, answer each multiple-choice question below. Then, count the number of times you used each letter as an answer (ABCD) to reveal a 4-digit code. Letters may be used more than once or not at all. If a letter option is not used, put a zero in that box.

1 Oglethorpe was granted a charter for land between what two rivers?

A. Ohio and Potomac Rivers
B. Missouri and Rio Grande Rivers
C. Mississippi and St. Johns Rivers
D. Savannah and Altamaha Rivers

2 Where were the Salzburgers originally from?

A. Norway
B. Russia
C. Spain
D. Austria

3 What city became Georgia's first settlement and capital?

A. Atlanta
B. Macon
C. Abbeville
D. Savannah

4 Oglethorpe, along with the first group of 120 settlers, arrived on what ship?

A. George
B. Anne
C. Nunes
D. None of the above

5 How many years did Oglethorpe serve as Georgia's governor?

A. 4 years
B. 8 years
C. 12 years
D. 16 years

6 The Battle of Bloody Marsh was fought between the British and who?

A. French Canada
B. French Louisiana
C. Spanish Florida
D. Spanish Texas

7 What groups made Georgia their home?

A. Scottish Highlanders
B. Methodists
C. Salzburgers
D. All of the above

8 What does the word "expelled" mean?

A. Money owed
B. Approved or enacted
C. Forced to leave
D. Small farms

Count how many times you used each letter as a correct answer (ABCD) to determine the 4-digit code. Record your answer in the boxes below.

# of A's | # of B's | # of C's | # of D's

MULTIPLE CHOICE

After reading the passage, answer each multiple-choice question. Then, count how many times you used each letter as a correct answer (ABCD) to determine the 4-digit code. Letters may be used more than once or not at all. If a letter option is not used, put a zero in that box. **Example: B,C,C,D,C,A,A,C = 2141** (The A was chosen as a correct answer for 2 questions, the B was chosen 1 time, C was used 4 times and D was chosen as a correct answer 1 time)

13 COLONIES

NEW ENGLAND COLONIES

A colony is a territory governed and controlled by a distant country. Often, the ruling country is located far from the colony itself, making direct oversight challenging. This was true for England and its American colonies, where England exercised political control over regions across the Atlantic, despite the great physical distance between them.

Queen Elizabeth sought to establish colonies in the Americas as a way to expand the British Empire and compete with Spain's growing influence in the New World. The English aimed to discover new sources of wealth, create job opportunities for their people, and set up trade ports along the coast.

The First Settlements

The New England Colonies included New Hampshire, Massachusetts Bay, Rhode Island, and Connecticut. These colonies were among the first settlements in North America. The New England Colonies were part of a larger group of thirteen that would later unite to form the United States. Situated along the northeastern coast, the New England region was characterized by its cold winters, rocky soil, and coastline, making it well-suited for fishing, whaling, and trade, though less ideal for farming.

In New England, a common practice known as the "triangular trade" emerged among shippers. They would transport rum to the coast of Africa, where it was exchanged for enslaved people. These enslaved individuals were then sold in the West Indies in exchange for molasses, which would be brought back to New England to produce more rum, continuing the cycle.

Why Did People Come to the New England Colonies?

Many came to the New England Colonies seeking religious freedom. In the 1600s, England was experiencing religious turmoil (chaos). Many religious groups, such as the Puritans and Pilgrims, faced persecution (treated harshly) for their beliefs. These groups wanted to create communities where they could practice their faith without interference from the English crown or the Anglican Church.

One of the earliest groups to arrive in New England were the Pilgrims, who sailed on the Mayflower in 1620 and established Plymouth Colony in present-day Massachusetts. The Pilgrims (also known as separatists) sought to separate entirely from the Church of England and build a society based on their religious beliefs. As the governor of Plymouth, William Bradford helped the Pilgrims survive their early years in New England, including enduring a harsh winter that nearly wiped out the settlement. His leadership and diplomacy with Native American groups, like the Wampanoag, were vital for the colony's survival.

Puritans founded the Massachusetts Bay Colony in 1630 under the leadership of John Winthrop. Unlike the Pilgrims, the Puritans wanted to reform the Church of England rather than separate from it entirely. Religious disagreements in the Massachusetts Colony led many non-Puritans to seek refuge elsewhere, prompting them to establish new settlements in Rhode Island and Connecticut in 1636, where there was greater religious tolerance.

Connecticut was founded by Thomas Hooker who brought one hundred members of his congregation with him. Rhode Island was founded by Roger Williams, a Puritan minister, and Anne Hutchinson after they were exiled (forced to leave) for their religious beliefs. Rhode Island became a place for Puritans and Quakers to express religious beliefs publicly. Although first settled in 1623 when John Mason received a land grant to establish a fishing colony, New Hampshire became a royal province in 1679.

Religion was the cornerstone of life in the New England Colonies. Most towns had a church at their center, and attendance at religious services was mandatory.

Arrival of English Settlers

The arrival of English settlers in New England dramatically changed the lives of Native American groups in the region. Initial relationships between colonists and Native Americans were often cooperative, especially in the early years when the settlers needed help with farming and surviving the winter. However, as more colonists arrived and expanded their settlements, tensions grew, leading to conflicts like King Philip's War in 1675. This war, led by the Wampanoag chief Metacom (King Philip), was one of the bloodiest conflicts between colonists and Native Americans, ultimately resulting in the defeat of the native groups and further expansion of English settlements.

The English often imposed their laws and practices on the Native Americans, including efforts to convert them to Christianity. Additionally, economic pressures and changing trade relationships disrupted the traditional ways of life for the natives. The Wampanoag and other groups grew frustrated with the loss of land, independence, and resources, which eventually led Metacom to unite with other Native American groups to push back against the English. By August 1676, the tide had turned against Metacom and his followers. The colonists systematically destroyed Native American villages, food supplies, and resources.

TRUE OR FALSE

After reading about the **New England Colonies**, read each statement below and determine if it is true or false. If the statement is true, color the coin that corresponds with that question. If the statement is false, cross out that coin value. When you are finished, add the TOTAL of **ALL TRUE** coin values to reveal a 4-digit code. One digit of the code has been provided for you. If the total is 625, a 6 would go in the first box, the 2 in the second box and so on.

A. The English often imposed their laws and practices on the Native Americans.

B. In the 1600s, England was experiencing religious turmoil (chaos).

C. As the governor of Plymouth, John Mason helped the Pilgrims survive their early years in New England.

D. The New England Colonies included Maine, Pennsylvania, Ohio, and Connecticut.

E. Rhode Island was founded by William Bradford.

F. Religion was the cornerstone of life in the New England Colonies.

G. The Pilgrims sought to separate entirely from the Church of England.

H. Rhode Island became a place for Puritans and Quakers to express religious beliefs publicly.

After shading the coins based on your answer, add the value of ALL TRUE statements to get the final total. Record your answer in the boxes below.

DOUBLE PUZZLE

After reading about the **New England Colonies**, determine the word that corresponds with the statements provided below. Spell the corresponding word in the boxes to the right. You may or may not use all squares provided for each answer. Any numerical answers must be spelled out. Next, use the numbers **under** indicated letters to reveal a secret word.

1	Last name of the founder of Connecticut					2				
2	Wampanoag chief during King Philip's War									
3	Last name of the founder of Rhode Island		4							
4	A territory governed and controlled by a distant country									
5	Wanted to reform the Church of England							8		
6	Forced to leave			6						
7	Name of the ship the Pilgrims sailed on					3				
8	Last name of the governor of Plymouth						7			
9	New Hampshire became a ___ province in 1679	1								
10	Also known as separatists				5					

SECRET WORD

1	2	3	4	5	6	7	8

MIDDLE COLONIES

The Middle Colonies, made up of New York, New Jersey, Pennsylvania, and Delaware, played a crucial role in shaping the early history of Colonial America. Known for their diverse populations, rich soil, and strategic location, these colonies became an economic powerhouse in the New World. They offered a mix of agriculture, industry, and trade that set them apart from both the New England and Southern colonies.

In 1609, Henry Hudson navigated up the Hudson River to Albany, New York, and explored the Delaware Bay on behalf of the Dutch East India Company. Between 1610 and 1616, the Dutch conducted further exploration and mapping expeditions. In 1613, they established their first colonies, and by 1614, the territory known as New Netherland marked the beginning of Dutch influence in the region.

Founding of the Middle Colonies

New York was originally settled by the Dutch as New Netherland in 1626. New York City, at that time, was called New Amsterdam. The area later came under English control in 1664. King Charles II granted the land to his brother, the Duke of York, after defeating the Dutch, thus renaming it New York. The colony became a vital center for trade due to its excellent harbor at the mouth of the Hudson River.

The English captured the Dutch territory of New Netherland, and part of this area was split off to form New Jersey around 1665. It was originally divided into East Jersey and West Jersey, but the two were reunited as a single royal colony by Queen Anne in 1702. Edward Hyde was appointed (chosen) the first governor of the royal colony. The fertile land made New Jersey an ideal spot for farming, attracting settlers from various backgrounds.

In 1681, William Penn, a Quaker, received a land grant from King Charles II to settle a debt owed to Penn's father. Penn envisioned Pennsylvania as a haven (safe place) for religious freedom and tolerance, particularly for Quakers, but also for other persecuted religious groups. Under Penn's leadership, Pennsylvania grew rapidly and became one of the most prosperous colonies in America. William Penn's charter guaranteed freedom of religion, promoted religious tolerance and democratic governance. Quakers, Catholics, Jews, Lutherans, and other religious minorities found a place to worship freely in the Middle Colonies.

Originally part of Pennsylvania, Delaware was founded by Peter Minuit and the New Sweden Company in 1638. The first permanent European settlement in Delaware was named Fort Christina, and the region became known as New Sweden. Delaware later came under English control in 1664. The region shared much of its early governance with Pennsylvania but eventually developed its own identity. In 1682, the Duke of York granted Delaware, then referred to as the Three Lower Counties, to William Penn, integrating it into the Pennsylvania Province. Although the counties in Delaware established their own assembly in 1704, they continued to operate under the governance of the Pennsylvania governor.

Economy of the Middle Colonies

The Middle Colonies developed a diverse economy that was vital to the colonial American economy as a whole. Known as the "breadbasket" colonies, their fertile soil and moderate climate allowed for the large-scale production of grains like wheat, barley, and rye, which were exported to other colonies and Europe.

The rich soil in the Middle Colonies supported a wide range of crops, making farming highly productive. Farmers typically produced enough for their own families while having surplus crops to sell or trade. Unlike the small farms in New England, many farms in the Middle Colonies were larger, with some using enslaved labor or indentured servants to aid in production.

The central location of the Middle Colonies made them ideal hubs for trade and commerce. Ports such as Philadelphia and New York City grew into major centers for importing and exporting goods. These ports facilitated trade not only between the colonies but also with Europe, Africa, and the Caribbean. Delaware's rivers provided routes for transporting goods to larger trading hubs like Philadelphia. The growth of shipbuilding and trading companies in these colonies further signified their economic importance.

The Middle Colonies also developed a thriving industry of skilled craftspeople. Blacksmiths, coopers, and carpenters set up shops in the growing towns and cities, contributing to a strong local economy. Traditionally, blacksmiths worked with iron and steel to create a variety of items, including tools, horseshoes, weapons, and decorative objects. Coopers specialized in making and repairing wooden containers known as barrels, casks, and tubs. Carpenters built homes, barns, bridges, and other infrastructures necessary for daily life. Small manufacturing businesses, like those producing iron, textiles, and paper, also emerged in this region.

PARAGRAPH CODE

After reading about the **Middle Colonies**, head back to the reading and number ALL the paragraphs in the reading passage. Then, read each statement below and determine which paragraph **NUMBER** the statement can be found in. Paragraph numbers MAY be used more than one time or not at all. Follow the directions below to reveal the 4-digit code.

A The first permanent European settlement in Delaware was named Fort Christina, and the region became known as New Sweden.

B Edward Hyde was appointed (chosen) the first governor of the royal colony.

C These ports facilitated trade not only between the colonies but also with Europe, Africa, and the Caribbean.

D They offered a mix of agriculture, industry, and trade that set them apart from both the New England and Southern colonies.

E In 1609, Henry Hudson navigated up the Hudson River to Albany, New York, and explored the Delaware Bay on behalf of the Dutch East India Company.

F Farmers typically produced enough for their own families while having surplus crops to sell or trade.

G New York was originally settled by the Dutch as New Netherland in 1626.

H William Penn's charter guaranteed freedom of religion, promoted religious tolerance and democratic governance.

ELIMINATE ALL EVEN-NUMBERED paragraphs that you used as an answer. Record the remaining numbers (in the SAME order in which you recorded them above) in the boxes below.

MYSTERY WORD

After reading about the **Middle Colonies**, determine if each statement below is true or false. Color or shade the boxes of the **TRUE** statements. Next, unscramble the mystery word using the large letters of the **TRUE** statements.

Delaware was founded by Peter Minuit. **R**	Carpenters built homes, barns, bridges, and other infrastructures necessary for daily life. **E**	The first permanent European settlement in Delaware was named Fort Christina. **C**	The counties in Delaware established their own assembly in 1704. **L**
Delaware's rivers provided routes for transporting goods to larger hubs. **T**	In 1609, Francis Drake navigated up the Hudson River to Albany, New York. **S**	In 1681, William Penn, a Quaker, received a land grant from King Charles II. **U**	Queen Anne reunited East and West Jersey in 1702. **I**
Edward Hyde was appointed the first governor of the royal colony of Vermont. **D**	Middle Colonies included New York, Pennsylvania, New Jersey and Delaware. **R**	New York was originally settled by the German. **P**	Traditionally, blacksmiths worked with iron and steel. **U**
King Charles II granted the land to his brother, the Duke of York. **A**	William Penn's charter guaranteed freedom of religion. **G**	Delaware later came under English control in 1687. **B**	The poor soil in the Middle Colonies only supported a small range of crops. **O**

Unscramble the word using the large bold letters of only the **TRUE** statements.

SOUTHERN COLONIES

The Southern Colonies in Colonial America played a significant role in the development of early America. Their rich lands, favorable climate, and strategic coastal locations shaped their economy, social structure, and relations with Native Americans and European powers. This region included Virginia, Maryland, North Carolina, South Carolina, and Georgia.

Founding of the Southern Colonies

Jamestown, Virginia was the first permanent English settlement in America, established in 1607 by the Virginia Company of London. The settlers, including John Smith, aimed to find wealth through gold and other resources. Jamestown struggled initially due to harsh conditions, disease, and conflict with local Native Americans known as Powhatan. However, the introduction of tobacco farming by John Rolfe transformed Virginia into a profitable colony.

Maryland was founded by George Calvert, also known as Lord Baltimore, as a haven for English Catholics facing persecution in England. Before George Calvert could secure a charter for a new colony in a warmer climate, he passed away in 1632. The charter was granted to George's son, Cecil, who carried forward his father's vision. While many of the early settlers were Catholic, the colony soon attracted a significant number of Protestant settlers, creating tensions between the two groups. The Act of Toleration was introduced in 1649 as a way to guarantee that Catholics and Protestants could coexist. Maryland was named after Queen Henrietta Maria of England.

North Carolina was originally part of the Carolina colony, which King Charles II granted to a group of eight proprietors known as the Lords Proprietors in 1663. Settlers began moving into the area around 1653. The colony developed slowly due to its rugged coastline and lack of a major port. However, the settlers engaged in farming and timber production. North Carolina separated from South Carolina in 1712 and became a royal colony in 1729.

South Carolina, like its northern counterpart, was part of the grant to the Lords Proprietors. Charles Town (now Charleston) was established in 1670. South Carolina became known for its large farming estates known as plantations, which grew rice, sugarcane, and indigo. Charleston became a major port, making the colony a center for trade.

Georgia was founded by James Oglethorpe in 1732 as a place for debtors and poor people from England to start anew and as a buffer zone against Spanish Florida. Oglethorpe's vision included a ban on slavery initially, but the colony eventually adopted the plantation system, focusing on crops like rice and indigo. Georgia was the last of the thirteen colonies to be established.

Economy of the Southern Colonies

The Southern Colonies had an economy centered around agriculture, supported by the region's warm climate, long growing season, and fertile soil. These factors made the area ideal for the cultivation of cash crops that were in high demand in Europe. A cash crop is a crop that is grown primarily for sale rather than for personal consumption. Tobacco became the dominant cash crop in Virginia and Maryland. It required extensive labor and was highly profitable, leading to the establishment of large plantations.

The plantation system became the backbone of the Southern economy. Large estates were established along rivers, making it easier to transport goods to markets. The plantations relied heavily on the labor of enslaved Africans. Enslaved people were brought in large numbers to work on plantations, particularly after the decline of the indentured servant system. In the early years of the colonies, indentured servants were a primary labor source. Indentured servants were English immigrants that agreed to work off their debt (money owed for the trip to America) for four to seven years. By the late 1600s, enslaved laborers made up a significant portion of the population.

The Southern Colonies relied on trade with England and the Caribbean. Major ports like Charleston facilitated the export of tobacco, rice, and indigo to Europe. North Carolina, with extensive pine forests, became a leading producer of tar and turpentine, which were essential for shipbuilding.

While the large plantations focused on cash crops, many smaller farmers in the interior regions grew their own food, such as corn, beans, and livestock. This self-sufficient lifestyle was common among those who did not own large tracts of land.

Society in the Southern Colonies

Wealthy plantation owners held significant power and influence over the region's politics and economy. A small middle class included merchants, small farmers, and skilled craftsmen. The labor demands of large plantations significantly increased the use of enslaved Africans, leading to the growth of the transatlantic slave trade, or Triangular Trade.

MYSTERY MATCH

After reading about the **Southern Colonies**, draw a line from the left-hand column to make a match in the right-hand column. Your line should go through **ONE** letter. When you complete all the matches, use the letters with a line THROUGH them to unscramble a mystery word. You MUST start and end your line at the **arrow points**.

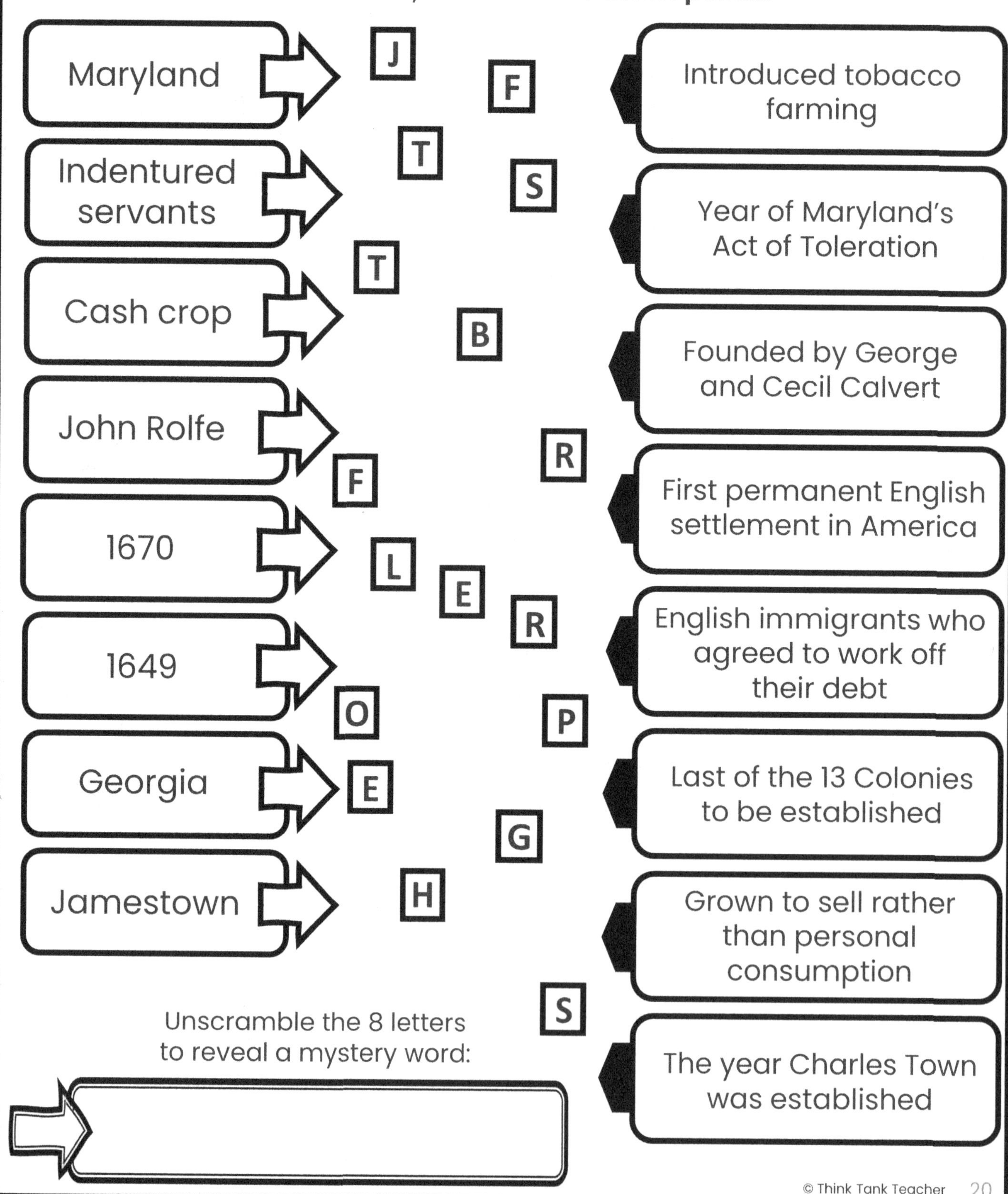

Maryland
Indentured servants
Cash crop
John Rolfe
1670
1649
Georgia
Jamestown
J
F
T
S
T
B
R
F
L
E
R
O
P
E
G
H
S
Introduced tobacco farming
Year of Maryland's Act of Toleration
Founded by George and Cecil Calvert
First permanent English settlement in America
English immigrants who agreed to work off their debt
Last of the 13 Colonies to be established
Grown to sell rather than personal consumption
The year Charles Town was established

Unscramble the 8 letters to reveal a mystery word:

MULTIPLE CHOICE

After reading about the **Southern Colonies**, answer each multiple-choice question below. Then, count the number of times you used each letter as an answer (ABCD) to reveal a 4-digit code. Letters may be used more than once or not at all. If a letter option is not used, put a zero in that box.

1 Which colony was founded by James Oglethorpe?

A. Maryland
B. Georgia
C. South Carolina
D. Virginia

2 Which colony, with extensive pine forests, became a leading producer of tar and turpentine?

A. Maryland
B. Georgia
C. Virginia
D. North Carolina

3 Who granted Carolina to the Lords Proprietors?

A. King George III
B. King James I
C. Queen Victoria
D. King Charles II

4 When was Jamestown established?

A. 1607
B. 1617
C. 1627
D. 1637

5 How long did indentured servants agree to work for to pay off their debt?

A. 1-3 years
B. 4-7 years
C. 8-11 years
D. 12-15 years

6 Who was known as Lord Baltimore?

A. George Calvert
B. John Rolfe
C. James Oglethorpe
D. John Smith

7 What was the transatlantic slave trade also known as?

A. Circular Trade
B. Triangular Trade
C. Linear Trade
D. Indentured Trade

8 Which colony was named after Queen Henrietta Maria?

A. Maryland
B. Georgia
C. Virginia
D. North Carolina

Count how many times you used each letter as a correct answer (ABCD) to determine the 4-digit code. Record your answer in the boxes below.

# of A's	# of B's	# of C's	# of D's

NEW ENGLAND COLONIES

PLYMOUTH

Pilgrims were settlers who came from Britain in search of religious freedom. Many Pilgrims were a part of a religious group called "Separatists." They wanted to separate from the Church of England, and so, they set sail to America in hopes of a new life. They wanted to be able to practice their religion how they wanted, without being persecuted (punished for their beliefs) like they were in Britain.

There were two ships the Pilgrims set sail on to America: the Mayflower and Speedwell. The Speedwell had a leak after it set sail, and they had to go back to England. They tried to put as many of the passengers from there onto the Mayflower. Most of them fit, but about twenty had to stay back because there was not enough room.

Setting Sail on the Mayflower

On September 6, 1620, the Mayflower set sail to America. There was a total of one-hundred-two passengers and about thirty crewmen. Some people just wanted a better life. Those passengers were called "strangers" and included merchants, skilled workers, and children. Less than half of the passengers aboard the vessel were Separatists. Captain Christopher Jones was commander of the Mayflower. Jones was an English merchant who purchased the ship in 1608.

The voyage across the Atlantic Ocean took two months to reach New England (known as America today). It was not an easy trip, with supplies running low, not enough fresh water, sickness, and storms. Two people died during the voyage. The original destination was Virginia, but storms took the ship off course, and they ended up landing near Cape Cod, Massachusetts.

Establishing Plymouth Colony

The Pilgrims named their new settlement 'New Plimouth' after the place in England that they set sail from. Once they reached land, the Pilgrims wanted to write and sign a document to determine how things would be decided and how issues would be settled. This document became known as the Mayflower Compact.

The goal of the document was to establish legal order. The Mayflower Compact included things such as their loyalty to the King, James I, their religion as Christianity, how they would work to help build the colony, and that their laws would be fair to all. Forty-one men from the Mayflower signed the Compact, as well as voted for a man named John Carver to be the first governor. Women and children were not allowed to sign the Mayflower Compact.

There were many reasons Plymouth was chosen for settlement. The colony had a harbor for their ship, a river for fresh water, and land that was flat for their crops.

Surviving the First Winter

The first winter in the new colony was not easy. The Pilgrims were not prepared for the bitter cold and had no shelter ready. As winter came, people had to sleep on the ship while they built a common house for everyone to stay in. Even then, the harsh winter was too much to handle and most of the Pilgrims lost their lives. By the end of the season, only forty-seven settlers remained from the original one-hundred-two. The governor, John Carver, also died after that winter, and a man named William Bradford was elected as the new governor.

One of the reasons some were able to survive was because of Native Americans in Plymouth, known as Wampanoag. When the Pilgrims arrived, the chief and the Pilgrims signed a treaty to maintain peace and to establish a trading relationship. One Native American, known as Squanto, knew some English since he had previously been in Europe. He stayed with the Pilgrims to help teach them how to plant corn, hunt, and fish. His assistance was crucial in adapting.

In 1621, the Pilgrims had their first harvest. In honor of that, they made a big feast and invited some of the Native Americans. This feast, which continues as tradition today, became known as Thanksgiving. Although people believe this dinner to be a happy time, no one knows if the Wampanoag enjoyed being there or were forced to attend. The story of Thanksgiving is often one-sided.

Before English colonists arrived in Plymouth, the Wampanoag had already been living on that land for more than 12,000 years. Many Pilgrims were seeking a place where they could live as they pleased, yet they did not extend that same concept to the Wampanoag.

Due to disease brought by Europeans, entire Wampanoag villages were wiped out. Expanding English settlements meant more intrusion on Native American lands. The Wampanoag realized that continued English presence meant a great threat to their way of life. Many people wrongly believe that the Pilgrims and Wampanoag coexisted in peace and harmony. Escalating tensions would later lead to King Philip's War. Today, descendants of Wampanoag worry their place in history is often forgotten.

TRUE OR FALSE

After reading about **Plymouth**, read each statement below and determine if it is true or false. If the statement is true, color the coin that corresponds with that question. If the statement is false, cross out that coin value. When you are finished, add the TOTAL of **ALL TRUE** coin values to reveal a 4-digit code. One digit of the code has been provided for you. If the total is 625, a 6 would go in the first box, the 2 in the second box and so on.

A. In 1621, the Pilgrims had their first harvest.

B. The voyage across the Atlantic Ocean took nine months to reach New England.

C. Due to disease brought by Europeans, entire Wampanoag villages were wiped out.

D. Captain William Bradford was commander of the Mayflower.

E. Many Pilgrims were a part of a religious group called "Separatists."

F. There was a total of one-hundred-two passengers and about thirty crewmen on the Mayflower.

G. There were two ships the Pilgrims set sail on to America: the Nina and the Pinta.

H. Women and children were not allowed to sign the Mayflower Compact.

After shading the coins based on your answer, add the value of ALL TRUE statements to get the final total. Record your answer in the boxes below.

DOUBLE PUZZLE

After reading about **Plymouth**, determine the word that corresponds with the statements provided below. Spell the corresponding word in the boxes to the right. You may or may not use all squares provided for each answer. Any numerical answers must be spelled out. Next, use the numbers **under** indicated letters to reveal a secret word.

#	Statement	Number under letter
1	The month the Mayflower set sail for America	4
2	Original destination of the Mayflower	6
3	Pilgrims set sail on two ships: the Mayflower and the ___	1
4	Last name of governor after John Carver passed away	8
5	Passengers who just wanted a better life	
6	Taught the pilgrims how to plant corn	5
7	The voyage across the ___ Ocean took two months	2
8	The Mayflower ___ established legal order	3
9	Last name of the Mayflower's captain	7
10	Separatists wanted to separate from the Church of ___	9

SECRET WORD

1	2	3	4	5	6	7	8	9

MASSACHUSETTS BAY

The Massachusetts Bay Colony formed the foundation for much of New England's development. Founded in 1630, it was established by a group of Puritans seeking religious freedom and the opportunity to build a society based on their beliefs. The colony grew quickly, becoming a hub for trade, education, and political influence in the region.

The idea for the Massachusetts Bay Colony began in England, where a group of Puritans, dissatisfied with the Church of England, sought to create a new society based on their religious principles. Unlike the Pilgrims of Plymouth, who were considered Separatists and wished to break away from the Church entirely, the Puritans of Massachusetts Bay sought to "purify" the Church while maintaining some ties to it. The Puritans were a group of Protestant Christians known for their strict religious beliefs and practices.

In 1629, King Charles I granted the Massachusetts Bay Company a charter which allowed the Puritans to establish a colony in the New World. The Massachusetts Bay Company was led by John Winthrop.

John Winthrop's Vision

John Winthrop, the first governor of the Massachusetts Bay Colony, played a crucial role in shaping the colony's direction. Before setting sail on the Arbella in 1630, Winthrop delivered a sermon in which he described his vision of the colony as a "city upon a hill." Winthrop named the colony after the Algonquin. The name "Massachusetts" translates to "at the great hill."

Winthrop and the other Puritan leaders believed that the Massachusetts Bay Colony should be a place where their religious ideals could flourish and where the community would be governed by their interpretation of Biblical principles. This vision influenced the strict social and legal codes that governed life in the colony.

Life in the Massachusetts Bay Colony

Life in the Massachusetts Bay Colony revolved around religion. The Puritans placed a strong emphasis on education, believing that everyone should be able to read the Bible. This commitment to learning led to the establishment of Harvard College in 1636, the first institution of higher education in the American colonies, aimed at training ministers.

The colony was organized into towns, each with a meetinghouse at its center, which served as both a place of worship and a town hall. The Puritan church and the government were closely linked, with only male church members allowed to vote or hold office. This close connection between the church and the government created a theocratic society, where religious leaders had power over everyday decisions and laws. In this kind of society, what the church said often influenced what happened in the community.

Despite the strictness of their society, the Massachusetts Bay Colony thrived due to its hardworking settlers and its location along the Atlantic coast, which was ideal for trade. The settlers engaged in fishing, farming, and shipbuilding. Though the rocky soil made large-scale agriculture difficult, the colony benefited from its proximity to the ocean, which provided fish and a means to trade with other colonies and England.

Tensions and Challenges

The Massachusetts Bay Colony faced various challenges, including internal disputes and conflicts with Native Americans. As the colony grew, tensions arose between the Puritan leadership and those who disagreed with their strict religious practices.

One famous dissenter was Roger Williams, who advocated (spoke up) for the separation of church and state and was banished (forced to leave) from the colony in 1636. A dissenter is a person who disagrees with the official beliefs and practices of a particular religion. Williams went on to found Rhode Island, which became known for its greater religious tolerance. Another dissenter, Anne Hutchinson, challenged the authority of the colony's ministers, leading to her trial and banishment in 1638.

Relations with Native Americans

The expansion of the Massachusetts Bay Colony led to increased interactions with Native Americans, particularly the Pequot and Wampanoag. At first, the relationship was one of cautious cooperation, as the settlers relied on Native American knowledge for survival and trade. However, as the Puritans expanded their settlements, competition for land and resources grew, leading to conflict.

The Pequot War in 1636-1638 was a significant conflict between the settlers and the Pequot, a Native American group that lived in what is now Connecticut. The Pequot had established trade relationships with the Dutch, which put them at odds with English settlers, who wanted to dominate trade in the area. The war ended with the near-destruction of the Pequot people, as Puritan forces attacked their villages. This war set a precedent for future conflicts between English settlers and Native Americans throughout New England, including King Philip’s War in the 1670s.

PARAGRAPH CODE

After reading about **Massachusetts Bay**, head back to the reading and number ALL the paragraphs in the reading passage. Then, read each statement below and determine which paragraph **NUMBER** the statement can be found in. Paragraph numbers MAY be used more than one time or not at all. Follow the directions below to reveal the 4-digit code.

A The Puritan church and the government were closely linked, with only male church members allowed to vote or hold office.

B Williams went on to found Rhode Island, which became known for its greater religious tolerance.

C In this kind of society, what the church said often influenced what happened in the community.

D The settlers engaged in fishing, farming, and shipbuilding.

E The name "Massachusetts" translates to "at the great hill."

F The Massachusetts Bay Colony formed the foundation for much of New England's development.

G The Puritans were a group of Protestant Christians known for their strict religious beliefs and practices.

H The Massachusetts Bay Colony faced various challenges, including internal disputes and conflicts with Native Americans.

ELIMINATE ALL EVEN-NUMBERED paragraphs that you used as an answer. Record the remaining numbers (in the SAME order in which you recorded them above) in the boxes below.

MYSTERY WORD

After reading about **Massachusetts Bay**, determine if each statement below is true or false. Color or shade the boxes of the **TRUE** statements. Next, unscramble the mystery word using the large letters of the **TRUE** statements.

Winthrop named the colony after the Algonquin. **H**	King Philip's War was fought by Spanish settlers and the French. **A**	The Pequot War took place from 1673-1675. **C**	The colony of Massachusetts Bay benefited from its proximity to the ocean. **R**
Roger Williams went on to found Rhode Island. **I**	Puritans were a strict group of Protestant Christians. **O**	The Massachusetts Bay Company was led by John Rolfe. **U**	Anne Hutchinson was banished in 1702. **L**
Only female church members allowed to vote or hold office. **E**	The Puritans placed a strong emphasis on education. **P**	Puritans of Massachusetts Bay sought to "purify" the Church. **T**	The name "Massachusetts" translates to "the upper house." **K**
Massachusetts Bay Colony was founded in 1607. **D**	Winthrop set sail on the Santa Maria in 1630. **M**	Harvard College was established in 1636. **W**	A dissenter is a person who disagrees with the official beliefs of a particular religion. **N**

Unscramble the word using the large bold letters of <u>only</u> the **TRUE** statements.

NEW HAMPSHIRE

The New Hampshire Colony can be traced back to 1623, when a group of fishermen from the region of Maine, led by Captain John Mason, John Wheelwright, and other English settlers, arrived in the area now known as New Hampshire. Captain Mason was granted a royal charter by King James I in 1629, officially recognizing New Hampshire as a separate entity from the Massachusetts Bay Colony.

The colony was established following the division of a land grant originally given in 1622. The Council for New England gave the grant to John Mason, a former governor of Newfoundland, and Sir Ferdinando Gorges, who founded Maine. Gorges took the land east of the Piscataqua River, calling it New Somersetshire, and Mason created the Province of New Hampshire to the south. Mason named the colony after the English county of Hampshire. Mason's vision was to create a prosperous colony based on agriculture and trade. He named the region "New Hampshire" after Hampshire, England, where he had previously lived. Mason died in 1635 before ever seeing the colony he founded.

Early Settlements and Challenges

The first settlers faced significant hardships upon their arrival. The Indigenous Abenaki people, who had lived in the area for generations, were initially wary of the newcomers. The settlers faced not only the physical challenges of the rugged terrain and harsh winters but also the complex dynamics of establishing relationships with the Native Americans. In the 1600s, when Europeans arrived, the region was home to various Algonquian peoples, including the Abenaki and Pennacook.

By the mid-1630s, as more families migrated from Massachusetts and other nearby colonies, the towns of Portsmouth, Dover, and Exeter emerged as some of the first established communities. Exeter, New Hampshire was founded by John Wheelwright in 1638. These towns served as centers for trade and social life. The settlers worked hard to adapt to their new environment, using techniques such as crop rotation and other agricultural practices to make the most of the rocky soil.

The settlers' relationship with the Abenaki people was complicated; initial interactions were often cooperative, involving trade and shared resources, but tensions eventually arose due to encroachments on Native lands. Encroachment refers to the gradual or unlawful intrusion or invasion into someone else's territory, rights, or property.

Economy of New Hampshire Colony

The economy of New Hampshire relied primarily on agriculture, fishing, timber, and trade. Due to the rocky soil and short growing season, large-scale farming was difficult. However, settlers managed to cultivate essential crops such as corn, wheat, barley, and oats. Livestock, including cattle and pigs, were also raised for food.

Fishing became a crucial part of the colony's economy, particularly as the settlers established themselves along the Atlantic coast. Cod, mackerel, and other fish were abundant, providing both sustenance and a commodity (product) for trade. Many families relied on the sea for their livelihoods.

Timber was another critical resource for the New Hampshire economy. The extensive forests provided wood for shipbuilding, construction, and fuel. As shipbuilding became increasingly important, towns like Portsmouth emerged as important shipbuilding centers.

Governance and Religious Life

In its early years, town meetings were a common way for settlers to discuss and make decisions about local issues. However, in 1679, New Hampshire was made a royal colony, directly controlled by the English monarchy. This transition meant that the governor was appointed (chosen) by the king, and a council was established to assist in governing the colony.

The religious landscape of New Hampshire was marked by diversity. Unlike other New England colonies, where one denomination (a distinct religious group) often dominated, New Hampshire allowed for various religious groups, including Puritans, Anglicans, Quakers, and others, to coexist.

The early settlers valued education and established schools to teach children. Religious education was also essential, with many communities forming congregational churches that became central to social life. The First Congregational Church of Portsmouth was established in 1638.

Conflicts Escalate

The encroachment of English settlers on Native lands and the spread of diseases brought by Europeans devastated Native populations. By the late 17th century, conflicts escalated, leading to King Philip's War, which significantly impacted both Native Americans and settlers in New England.

MYSTERY MATCH

After reading about **New Hampshire**, draw a line from the left-hand column to make a match in the right-hand column. Your line should go through **ONE** letter. When you complete all the matches, use the letters with a line THROUGH them to unscramble a mystery word. You MUST start and end your line at the **arrow points**.

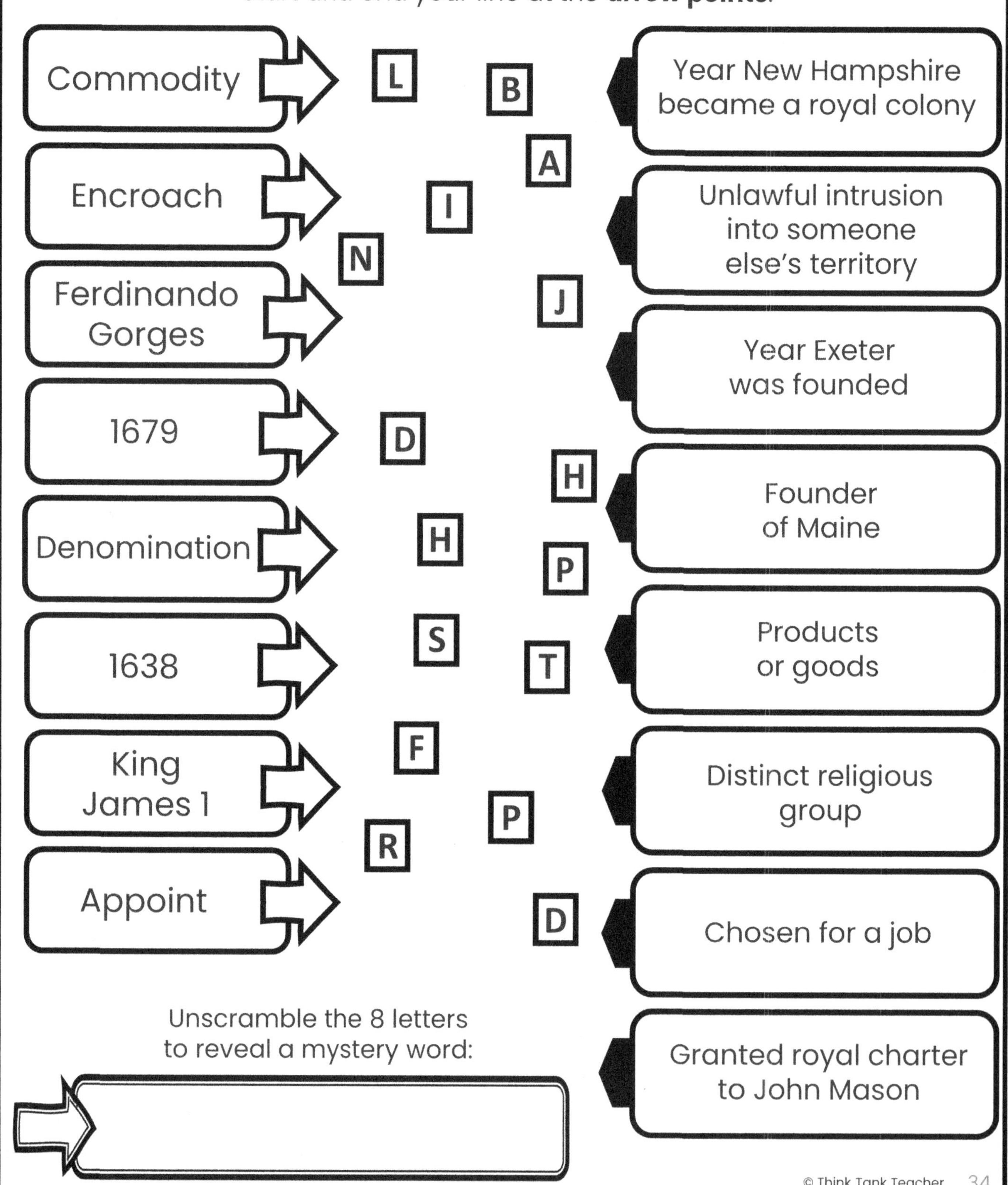

Unscramble the 8 letters to reveal a mystery word:

MULTIPLE CHOICE

After reading about **New Hampshire**, answer each multiple-choice question below. Then, count the number of times you used each letter as an answer (ABCD) to reveal a 4-digit code. Letters may be used more than once or not at all. If a letter option is not used, put a zero in that box.

1 What did the economy of New Hampshire rely on?

A. Fishing
B. Timber
C. Agriculture
D. All of the above

2 What did the extensive forests of New Hampshire provide wood for?

A. Construction
B. Fuel
C. Shipbuilding
D. All of the above

3 In the 1600s, when Europeans arrived, who was the New Hampshire region home to?

A. Abenaki
B. Pennacook
C. Algonquian
D. All of the above

4 Mason was the former governor of what region?

A. Providence
B. Exeter
C. Newfoundland
D. Jamestown

5 Mason and Gorges split the land based on what river?

A. Punxatawny River
B. Piscataqua River
C. Potomac River
D. None of the above

6 What religious groups settled in New Hampshire?

A. Quakers
B. Anglicans
C. Puritans
D. All of the above

7 When was Captain Mason granted a royal charter by King James I?

A. 1609
B. 1619
C. 1629
D. 1639

8 Who founded Exeter, New Hampshire?

A. Wheelwright
B. Gorges
C. Jones
D. Williams

Count how many times you used each letter as a correct answer (ABCD) to determine the 4-digit code. Record your answer in the boxes below.

# of A's	# of B's	# of C's	# of D's

CONNECTICUT

The Connecticut Colony was one of the original thirteen American colonies established by European settlers. Located in New England, it was known for its river valleys, harsh winters, and natural resources. The colony's history is deeply rooted in Puritan values and a desire for independence.

Dutch privateer Adriaen Block was the first European to explore Connecticut in 1614. During his expedition, Block and his crew navigated up the Connecticut River, creating maps of the area that would guide future Dutch settlers.

Before European settlement, Connecticut was inhabited by various Native American groups, including the Pequot, Mohegan, and Narragansett peoples. These native groups spoke the Algonquian language and named the local river "Quinnehtukqut," which means "land on the long tidal river."

Founding Connecticut

The Connecticut Colony was founded in 1636 when Thomas Hooker, a Puritan minister, led a group of settlers from the Massachusetts Bay Colony to the fertile area along the Connecticut River. They sought greater religious freedom and the opportunity to establish a community based on their own interpretation of Puritan beliefs. Hooker strongly supported the idea of universal Christian suffrage, meaning he believed that all Christians should have the right to vote, regardless of whether they were members of a specific church. Hooker's group settled in what would become Hartford, one of Connecticut's earliest settlements.

Other towns were soon established, including Windsor and Wethersfield, which joined Hartford in 1637 to form a unified government under the name "Connecticut." In 1662, the Connecticut Colony received a Royal Charter from the King of England.

Economy

Farming played a central role in Connecticut's economy. The fertile soil along the Connecticut River Valley made it possible for colonists to grow crops like wheat, corn, barley, and oats. Livestock such as cattle, pigs, and sheep were also raised. While farms in Connecticut were smaller than those in the Southern Colonies, they provided essential food for the settlers and surplus crops for trade.

The coastal location made fishing and whaling important industries. Fish, especially cod, were abundant, and whaling provided oil, which was used for lamps. Connecticut's dense forests provided timber, which was essential for building ships. These ships were used for trade, transporting goods like timber, livestock, and crops to other colonies and England. The colony also participated in the triangular trade, exchanging goods with the Caribbean, Africa, and Europe.

Religion

The settlers who founded Connecticut were primarily Puritans, a group of Protestants seeking to purify the Church of England from practices they considered too similar to Catholicism. Puritan beliefs emphasized hard work, community, and a strict moral code. Puritan values influenced the colony's laws and daily life. Attendance at church services was mandatory, and the church held significant authority over community matters.

Fundamental Orders

One of Connecticut's most significant contributions was the Fundamental Orders of Connecticut, adopted in 1639. This document outlined a framework for self-governance and is considered by many historians as the first written constitution in the New World. It established a government with an elected governor and a General Court, which included representatives from each town.

The Fundamental Orders did not require colonists to be members of the Puritan church in order to vote, which was a departure from practices in other Puritan colonies. Historians believe that the Fundamental Orders may have been drafted by Roger Ludlow. At the time, he was the only trained lawyer in Connecticut. Under the newly established constitution, John Haynes was chosen as the governor.

Pequot War

As more settlers moved into the Connecticut region, tensions grew with the local Native Americans. The Pequot, aiming to control the fur trade, often attacked other Indigenous groups that attempted to trade with the European settlers. Some traders resented the Pequot's dominance over the fur trade and decided to take action by capturing Tatobem, the Pequot chief, and holding him for ransom. However, the situation escalated when the traders killed the chief, leading to the outbreak of the Pequot War (1636-1638). After a series of brutal confrontations and outbreak of disease, the settlers ultimately emerged victorious, nearly wiping out the Pequot people in the process.

TRUE OR FALSE

After reading about **Connecticut**, read each statement below and determine if it is true or false. If the statement is true, color the coin that corresponds with that question. If the statement is false, cross out that coin value. When you are finished, add the TOTAL of **ALL TRUE** coin values to reveal a 4-digit code. One digit of the code has been provided for you. If the total is 625, a 6 would go in the first box, the 2 in the second box and so on.

A. In 1662, the Connecticut Colony received a Royal Charter from the King of England.

B. Under the newly established constitution, John Haynes was chosen as the governor.

C. The Fundamental Orders of Connecticut was adopted in 1687.

D. Puritan beliefs emphasized hard work, community, and a strict moral code.

E. Dutch privateer John Winthrop was the first European to explore Connecticut in 1602.

F. The Fundamental Orders required colonists to be members of the Puritan church in order to vote.

G. The Connecticut Colony was founded in 1636 by Thomas Hooker.

H. "Quinnehtukqut" means "land on the long tidal river."

After shading the coins based on your answer, add the value of ALL TRUE statements to get the final total. Record your answer in the boxes below.

DOUBLE PUZZLE

After reading about **Connecticut**, determine the word that corresponds with the statements provided below. Spell the corresponding word in the boxes to the right. You may or may not use all squares provided for each answer. Any numerical answers must be spelled out. Next, use the numbers **under** indicated letters to reveal a secret word.

#	Statement	Boxes (9)	Numbered box
1	Hooker believed all Christians should have the right to ___	□□□□□□□□□	6 (under box 4)
2	Attendance at church services was ___	□□□□□□□□□	
3	Pequot chief	□□□□□□□□□	
4	John Haynes was chosen as the ___	□□□□□□□□□	2 (under box 6)
5	"Quinnehtukqut" means "land on the long ___ river"	□□□□□□□□□	3 (under box 2)
6	___ provided oil, which was used for lamps	□□□□□□□□□	5 (under box 5)
7	The Fundamental ___ of Connecticut was adopted in 1639	□□□□□□□□□	7 (under box 3)
8	Last name of the only trained lawyer in Connecticut	□□□□□□□□□	1 (under box 2)
9	Last name of the first Dutch privateer to explore Connecticut	□□□□□□□□□	
10	Hooker's group settled in what would become ___	□□□□□□□□□	4 (under box 5)

SECRET WORD

1	2	3	4	5	6	7

RHODE ISLAND

The Rhode Island Colony was unique in its founding principles and became a place of refuge for those seeking religious freedom. Established in the 17th century, Rhode Island distinguished itself by embracing religious tolerance in a time when other colonies were much more restrictive.

Founders and Early History

Rhode Island was founded by Roger Williams in 1636. Williams, a religious dissenter, was originally a Puritan minister in the Massachusetts Bay Colony. However, he began to challenge the colony's leadership on several issues, including the separation of church and state, and the treatment of Native Americans. He believed that the government should not interfere with religious matters and that colonists should purchase land from Native Americans rather than simply taking it. These ideas made him a target, and he was banished (forced to leave) from Massachusetts Bay Colony in 1635.

After his banishment, Williams fled south and eventually settled near Narragansett Bay, where he purchased land from the Indigenous group known as Narragansett. This new settlement became Providence, the first town in what would become Rhode Island. In Providence, Williams set up a community based on his beliefs in religious freedom.

In 1637, a group of dissenters from Massachusetts bought land from Native Americans on Aquidneck Island and started a settlement called Pocasset. This group included William Coddington, John Clarke, and Anne Hutchinson, among others. Not long after, the settlement split into two. Coddington and Clarke went on to found the nearby settlement of Newport in 1639. Anne Hutchinson founded Portsmouth in 1638 after being banished from Massachusetts for her own religious views. Other settlements soon followed, including Warwick. These towns later united to form the Colony of Rhode Island and Providence Plantations in 1644 when Roger Williams obtained a charter from the English Parliament, allowing them to form a colony. In 1663, the colony was granted a new charter by King Charles II of England, uniting four settlements. The royal charter guaranteed religious freedom and allowed the colony to elect its own officials.

Economy

The economy of Rhode Island was diverse and took advantage of its coastal location. Early on, the colony's economy centered on farming, fishing, and trade. Settlers farmed crops like corn, wheat, and barley, while raising livestock such as cattle and pigs. Fishing and whaling also became important industries, with fish like cod and mackerel. The coastal waters made shipbuilding another key industry in the colony. Newport, in particular, became a bustling port, serving as a hub for trade between Europe, the Caribbean, and other colonies.

Rhode Island also played a controversial role in the triangular trade. Some of the colony's merchants participated in the trade of enslaved Africans, sending rum from Rhode Island to Africa, trading for enslaved people, and transporting them to the Caribbean and the Southern Colonies. This participation in the slave trade, though not the only source of the colony's prosperity, contributed to its wealth during this period.

Religion

Rhode Island became known for its religious freedom. Unlike other colonies that mandated adherence to a particular church, Rhode Island allowed people of various beliefs to worship as they chose. This made it a safe haven for groups like Quakers, Baptists, Jews, and others who faced persecution elsewhere in New England.

Roger Williams believed that religion should be a personal matter, and that the government had no right to enforce religious practices. This was a radical idea at the time when most colonies had established churches and required attendance at services. Williams's vision helped to shape Rhode Island into a place where dissenters from various religious backgrounds could coexist.

Relationship with Native Americans

One of Roger Williams's defining principles was his fair treatment of Native Americans. He believed that land should be purchased from Native Americans rather than taken by force. His approach led to relatively peaceful relations with the Narragansett and other Indigenous groups in the area during the early years of the colony.

However, this peaceful relationship was tested during King Philip's War (1675-1676), a conflict between Native Americans and New England colonists. Although Rhode Island tried to maintain neutrality, the war spread throughout the region, and the Narragansett eventually joined King Philip (Metacom) against the English settlers. The war resulted in significant destruction in Rhode Island, with Providence itself being burned.

PARAGRAPH CODE

After reading about **Rhode Island**, head back to the reading and number ALL the paragraphs in the reading passage. Then, read each statement below and determine which paragraph **NUMBER** the statement can be found in. Paragraph numbers MAY be used more than one time or not at all. Follow the directions below to reveal the 4-digit code.

A Anne Hutchinson founded Portsmouth in 1638 after being banished from Massachusetts for her own religious views.

B One of Roger Williams's defining principles was his fair treatment of Native Americans.

C Rhode Island also played a controversial role in the triangular trade.

D Williams, a religious dissenter, was originally a Puritan minister in the Massachusetts Bay Colony.

E The coastal waters made shipbuilding another key industry in the colony.

F The war resulted in significant destruction in Rhode Island, with Providence itself being burned.

G Settlers farmed crops like corn, wheat, and barley, while raising livestock such as cattle and pigs.

H This made it a safe haven for groups like Quakers, Baptists, Jews, and others who faced persecution elsewhere in New England.

ELIMINATE ALL EVEN-NUMBERED paragraphs that you used as an answer. Record the remaining numbers (in the SAME order in which you recorded them above) in the boxes below.

MYSTERY WORD

After reading about **Rhode Island**, determine if each statement below is true or false. Color or shade the boxes of the **TRUE** statements. Next, unscramble the mystery word using the large letters of the **TRUE** statements.

Rhode Island allowed people of various beliefs to worship as they chose. **N**	Providence was burned during King Philip's War. **I**	King Philip was also known as Tatobem. **P**	Williams fled north and settled near Chesapeake Bay after being banished. **M**
Narragansett eventually joined King Philip against the English settlers. **T**	In 1663, the colony was granted a new charter by King Charles II of England. **S**	Williams purchased land from the Narragansett. **S**	Rhode Island was founded by Roger Williams in 1636. **E**
Williams was originally a Puritan minister in the Georgia Colony. **J**	King Philip's War took place from 1775-1776. **F**	To be banished means forced to leave. **S**	Early on, the colony's economy centered on farming, fishing, and trade. **E**
Coddington and Clarke went on to found the settlement of Newport in 1639. **D**	Roger Williams believed that religion should be a personal matter. **R**	Anne Hutchinson founded Warwick in 1632. **B**	Rhode Island was established in the late 15th century. **C**

Unscramble the word using the large bold letters of <u>only</u> the **TRUE** statements.

SALEM WITCH TRIALS

During the 15th and 16th centuries, belief in the supernatural and fear of witchcraft were widespread in Europe. This fear crossed the Atlantic with early European settlers and became a part of life in the New England colonies. Many Puritans, strict Christians who settled in Massachusetts, believed that the devil could work through witches to harm communities. They saw any signs of the supernatural as direct threats to their way of life.

In 1641, an English law officially declared witchcraft as a capital crime. The punishment would be burning at the stake. Decades later, there was still a fear of witches and their power to harm people through dark magic.

Witchcraft Accusations

During the spring of 1692, a group of young girls claimed to be possessed by the devil and pointed fingers at several women whom they claimed were witches. This began one of the most infamous six months in Salem, which is today well-known as the Salem Witch Trials. During this time, hundreds of people were accused of practicing witchcraft. It all began in the Parris household when Betty Parris and her cousin began twitching, twisting, and make strange noises.

Rising Fear

In 1692, a group of young girls fell sick after reading their fortunes and began to behave in a very strange manner. Fortune-telling games were forbidden by the Puritans. Seven girls around the ages of nine and twelve were diagnosed by a local doctor. The girls, known as the "afflicted," were screaming, having convulsions, and making strange or destructive movements with their bodies. The girls also had a high fever and were often in a trance-like state. Doctor William Griggs, baffled by the behaviors, diagnosed the girls as having been bewitched.

The fear spread quickly through Salem Village as more girls exhibited similar symptoms. With no medical explanation available, the community turned to the idea that they were being bewitched. Pressured by adults, the afflicted girls began accusing various women of causing their afflictions through witchcraft. With all the hysteria of who might or might not be a witch and what they might or might not do to a person to hurt them or keep them silent, everyone was afraid. Most people sided with the accusers, and the so-called witches were brought to trial.

In February, the afflicted girls accused their first three victims of witchcraft and those women were soon arrested. One of the arrested was a woman named Tituba, the slave of Pastor Parris. Another woman arrested was a homeless beggar named Sarah Good. The third woman arrested was a poor, older woman named Sarah Osborn. At the trial, when the three accused witches entered the courtroom, some of the afflicted girls had convulsions and began screaming. Sarah Good and Sarah Osborne proclaimed their innocence, but Tituba confessed under pressure, likely hoping to save herself from punishment.

Unfair Trials and More Accusations

Governor William Phips created a special court, known as the Court of Oyer and Terminer, to hear the witchcraft cases. The court allowed "spectral evidence," which meant that dreams, visions, and the claims of the afflicted could be used as evidence of witchcraft. This type of evidence, impossible to prove or disprove, made it nearly impossible for the accused to defend themselves. The trials were unfair and incredibly cruel.

The women accused of witchcraft could lessen their punishment by naming other witches. Some did, and even more women were brought into the trials. A woman named Bridget Bishop was accused of witchcraft on June 2nd. Eight days later, she was hanged. She was the first person executed in Salem. Over the next three months, eighteen more women accused of witchcraft were hanged on Gallows Hill. Eight women died while in jail. Sarah Osborn's husband was stoned to death because he refused to say whether he was innocent or guilty.

Reverend Cotton Mather spoke against convicting women on 'spectral evidence' or judging based on what you see. It was assumed that people were witches because of convulsions or screaming behaviors exhibited by others. Mather argued for due process, meaning he expected the same kind of evidence used in a regular trial to apply to witch trials as well. The governor of Salem agreed that any future trials would require tangible evidence before conviction. In all but one case, those accused of witchcraft were found guilty at trial and condemned to death. The people of Salem began to realize that innocent people were being sentenced to death.

An eighty-year-old farmer named Giles Corey was pressed to death by heavy stones. He refused to say if he was innocent or guilty. The last of the witchcraft trials were held in May of 1693. In May, all those in jail on the charge of witchcraft were pardoned and released by the governor. Once pardoned from jail, the Commonwealth of Massachusetts paid each victim six-hundred British Pounds.

MYSTERY MATCH

After reading about the **Salem Witch Trials**, draw a line from the left-hand column to make a match in the right-hand column. Your line should go through **ONE** letter. When you complete all the matches, use the letters with a line THROUGH them to unscramble a mystery word. You MUST start and end your line at the **arrow points**.

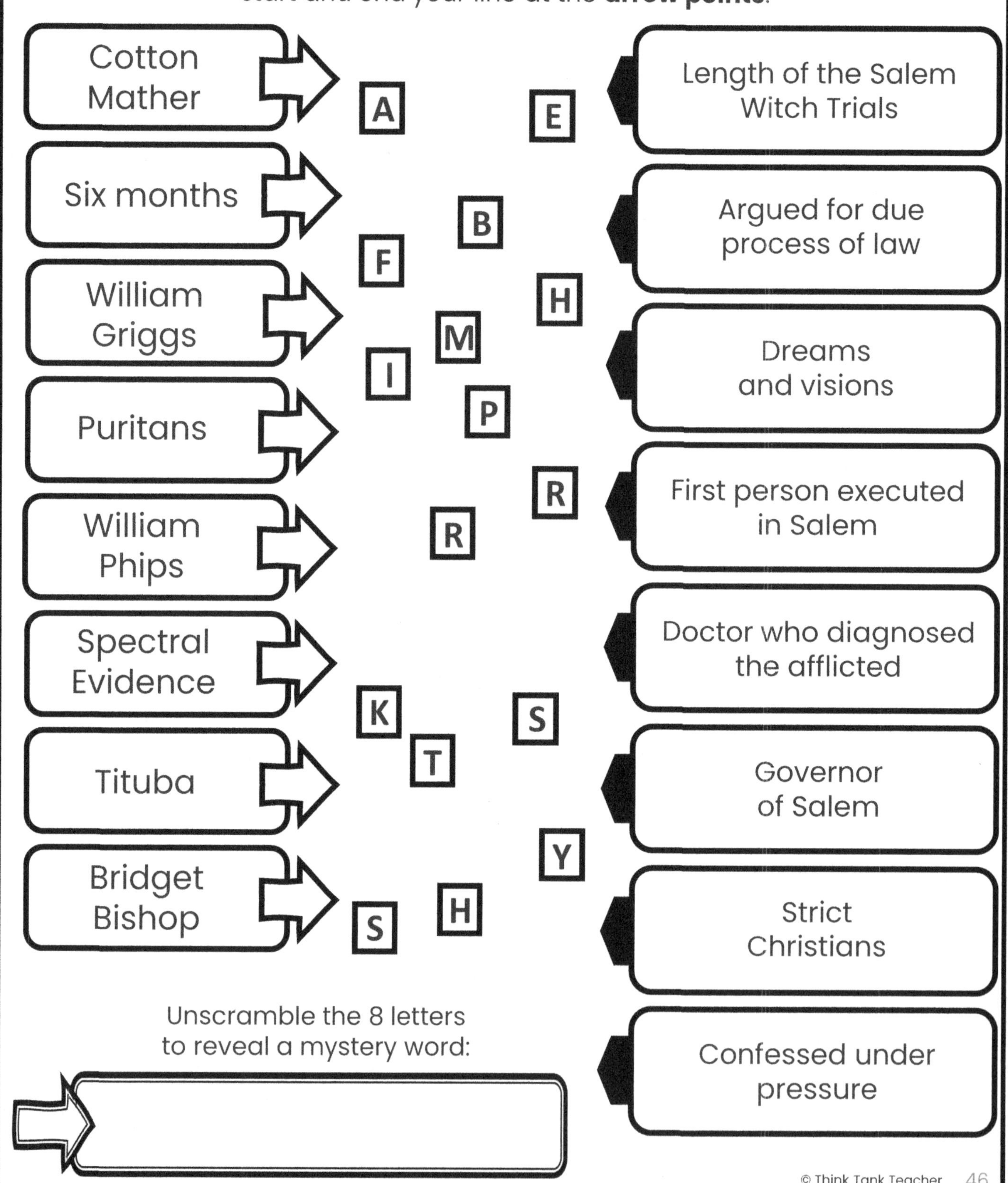

Cotton Mather
Six months
William Griggs
Puritans
William Phips
Spectral Evidence
Tituba
Bridget Bishop
A
E
B
F
H
M
I
P
R
R
K
S
T
Y
S
H
Length of the Salem Witch Trials
Argued for due process of law
Dreams and visions
First person executed in Salem
Doctor who diagnosed the afflicted
Governor of Salem
Strict Christians
Confessed under pressure

Unscramble the 8 letters to reveal a mystery word:

MULTIPLE CHOICE

After reading about the **Salem Witch Trials**, answer each multiple-choice question below. Then, count the number of times you used each letter as an answer (ABCD) to reveal a 4-digit code. Letters may be used more than once or not at all. If a letter option is not used, put a zero in that box.

1 What were the special witchcraft courts known as?

A. Court of Common Pleas
B. Court of Exchequer
C. Court of Oyer and Terminer
D. None of the above

2 When were the last of the witchcraft trials held?

A. May of 1693
B. June of 1691
C. May of 1697
D. June of 1672

3 In what household did the hysteria of witchcraft begin?

A. Griggs household
B. Mather household
C. Osborn household
D. Parris household

4 Who spoke against convicting women on 'spectral evidence'?

A. Pastor Parris
B. Sarah Osborn
C. Reverend Mather
D. William Griggs

5 What did the afflicted girls do?

A. Twitch
B. Twist their bodies
C. Make strange noises
D. All of the above

6 When did an English law officially declare witchcraft as a capital crime?

A. 1641
B. 1651
C. 1661
D. 1671

7 Who was a homeless beggar arrested for witchcraft?

A. Sarah Good
B. Tituba
C. Sarah Osborn
D. Cotton Mather

8 Once pardoned from jail, how much was each victim paid?

A. Six-hundred British Pounds
B. Twelve-hundred Pesos
C. Fourteen-hundred British Pounds
D. Twenty-four-hundred Pesos

Count how many times you used each letter as a correct answer (ABCD) to determine the 4-digit code. Record your answer in the boxes below.

# of A's	# of B's	# of C's	# of D's

MIDDLE COLONIES

NEW YORK

The New York Colony, initially founded as New Netherland by the Dutch in the early 17th century, became a cornerstone of economic, cultural, and political life in early America. It was a diverse colony that served as a melting pot of different cultures, religions, and economic activities.

Founding and Early History

Most European explorers of the New Land were looking for the legendary Northwest Passage, a water route to Asia, or gold and silver. New York's roots trace back to 1609, when Henry Hudson, an English explorer working for the Dutch East India Company, sailed up what is now known as the Hudson River. His ship was called the "Halve Maen" or New Moon. The Dutch West India Company, a trading company from the Netherlands, was granted a monopoly. This meant that it was only company allowed to trade in West Africa and the Americas for the Dutch.

Hudson's exploration paved the way for Dutch settlers, who established trading posts and small settlements in the region. In 1614, Fort Nassau (now Albany) became the first Dutch settlement in North America. By 1624, the Dutch had sent thirty families to the region and officially founded the colony of New Netherland, focusing on fur trading and forming alliances with local Native American groups like the Mohawk and Iroquois.

The Dutch West India Company took control of the colony and established the town of New Amsterdam (New York City) on the southern tip of Manhattan Island in 1626. Peter Minuit of New Netherland purchased Manhattan Island from the local Lenape people for goods valued at $24. Fairness of this transaction remain a point of debate among historians.

To encourage the growth of their colony, the Dutch West India Company created the "Charter of Freedoms and Exemptions," which introduced the Patroon System. This system allowed wealthy investors, called "Patroons," to receive large pieces of land if they brought fifty settlers and their families to New Netherland. In exchange, the Patroons were given large land tracts along the Hudson River and acted like landlords, managing the families living on their property.

Transition to English Control

In 1664, during a period of rivalry between the Dutch and the English, King Charles II of England granted the land of New Netherland to his brother James, the Duke of York, even though it was already occupied by the Dutch.

An English fleet arrived at New Amsterdam and demanded its surrender. Lacking adequate military defense, Dutch Governor Peter Stuyvesant was forced to surrender the colony to Richard Nicolls without a fight. The colony was renamed New York in honor of the Duke of York. Nicolls went on to become the first governor of New York.

Economy of New York Colony

New York quickly grew into one of the most prosperous colonies due to its strategic location along the Atlantic coast. The economy was built on agriculture, trade, and shipping. The fertile soil of the Hudson Valley allowed farmers to grow a variety of crops, including wheat, barley, and corn. Wheat, in particular, became an important export, earning New York the nickname "the breadbasket colony." Farmers also raised livestock such as cattle and pigs, providing both food for the colony and products for export. Natural resources included coal, furs, forestry (timber), and iron ore.

The port of New York became one of the busiest in the colonies, attracting merchants from Europe, the Caribbean, and other American colonies. Ships loaded with agricultural products, furs, and other goods regularly left New York's ports for European markets, while imports of finished goods, sugar, and rum flowed in.

Religion and Diversity

Unlike some of the other colonies, New York did not have an official church and offered a degree of religious freedom. This made it a welcoming destination for people of various beliefs and backgrounds, allowing different faiths to coexist. The colony was home to many religious groups, including Anglicans, Quakers, Lutherans, Jews, and Dutch Reformed Church members. Dutch, English, German, French, and Scandinavian settlers, as well as enslaved Africans, all contributed to the colony's population.

Relations with Native Americans

Initially, the Dutch and later the English engaged in fur trade with the Iroquois Confederacy and other Natives. The Iroquois formed a group called the Five Nations, made up of five Indigenous groups: the Mohawk, Oneida, Cayuga, Onondaga, and Seneca. The fur trade created alliances, but it also led to conflicts over land and control of resources. As the English expanded their control, they began to push Native American groups off their ancestral lands, leading to the displacement of many Natives.

TRUE OR FALSE

After reading about **New York**, read each statement below and determine if it is true or false. If the statement is true, color the coin that corresponds with that question. If the statement is false, cross out that coin value. When you are finished, add the TOTAL of **ALL TRUE** coin values to reveal a 4-digit code. One digit of the code has been provided for you. If the total is 625, a 6 would go in the first box, the 2 in the second box and so on.

A. As the English expanded their control, they began to push Native American groups off their ancestral lands.

B. Peter Minuit purchased Manhattan Island from the local Lenape people for goods valued at $24.

C. Henry Hudson went on to become the first governor of New York.

D. Hudson's ship was called the "Pinta" or New Surface.

E. The New York Colony was initially founded as New Nassau by the French.

F. New York quickly grew into one of the most prosperous colonies due to its strategic location along the Pacific coast.

G. In 1614, Fort Bronx became the first Dutch settlement in North America.

H. Most European explorers of the New Land were looking for the legendary Northwest Passage.

After shading the coins based on your answer, add the value of ALL TRUE statements to get the final total. Record your answer in the boxes below.

			9

DOUBLE PUZZLE

After reading about **New York**, determine the word that corresponds with the statements provided below. Spell the corresponding word in the boxes to the right. You may or may not use all squares provided for each answer. Any numerical answers must be spelled out. Next, use the numbers **under** indicated letters to reveal a secret word.

#	Statement	Boxes / Number under letter
1	New ___ is now present-day New York City	
2	Last name of New Netherland's person that purchased Manhattan Island	3 (under box 3)
3	Synonym for forestry	
4	The legendary ___ Passage was a water route to Asia	4 (under box 2)
5	First name of the Duke of York	1 (under box 3)
6	Fort Nassau is now this present-day city in New York	7 (under box 2), 8 (under box 6)
7	Wealthy investors who received large pieces of land if they brought fifty settlers	6 (under box 5)
8	The Iroquois formed a group called the Five ___	2 (under box 5)
9	First name of Dutch Governor Stuyvesant	5 (under box 1)
10	Dutch West ___ Company	

SECRET WORD

1	2	3	4	5	6	7	8

NEW JERSEY

New Jersey was a colony marked by diversity, religious tolerance, and economic opportunity. Its strategic location, fertile land, and welcoming environment for people of different backgrounds made it an appealing destination for settlers seeking a new life in America.

The first permanent European settlement in the region was founded by the Dutch at Bergen (present-day Jersey City) in 1660. New Jersey Colony was founded in 1664 after the English seized the area from the Dutch. Woodbridge, settled in the fall of 1664, is the oldest township in New Jersey.

Land Grants

King Charles II of England granted the land to his brother, James, the Duke of York. Soon after, the Duke of York (later King James II) gifted the territory between the Hudson and Delaware Rivers to two of his loyal friends, Sir George Carteret and Lord John Berkeley. This region would be named "New Jersey" in honor of Carteret, who had previously served as governor of the Isle of Jersey in England.

Carteret and Berkeley planned to attract settlers by offering generous terms, such as land grants, religious freedom, and self-governance. The "Concession and Agreement" was a document granting religious freedom to all inhabitants of New Jersey. The men divided the land into two parts - East Jersey and West Jersey - each governed separately for a time.

In exchange for land, settlers in New Jersey were required to pay annual fees called quitrents. Additionally, land grants linked to the importation of enslaved people served as another incentive for settlers to move to the colony. Philip Carteret, appointed by the two proprietors (owners), became the first governor of the proprietary colony. However, the collection of quitrents later proved to be a challenge. As a result, in March of 1673, Sir John Berkeley sold his share of New Jersey to the Quakers.

East Jersey's capital was Perth Amboy and Burlington served as the capital of West Jersey. These divisions later unified into a single colony in 1702, coming under direct control of the English crown as a royal colony. New Jersey's first royal colonial governor was Edward Hyde, also known as Lord Cornbury.

Economy of the New Jersey Colony

The economy of New Jersey was largely agricultural, but the region also benefited from its strategic location between New York and Pennsylvania, making it an important hub for trade and commerce. The favorable climate allowed for successful farming, and settlers grew crops such as wheat, corn, barley, oats, and rye. This led to New Jersey being known as part of the "Breadbasket Colonies," along with New York, Delaware, and Pennsylvania.

The colony also had a prosperous iron industry, producing items like tools, nails, and kettles. The abundance of forests in the region provided materials for shipbuilding, which became another significant industry.

Religion in New Jersey Colony

New Jersey welcomed settlers of various faiths. This was a major draw for people escaping religious persecution in Europe, such as Quakers, Baptists, Presbyterians, and Dutch Reformed groups. Lord John Berkeley sold his share of West Jersey to Quaker investors, including William Penn, which attracted many Quaker settlers to the area. The Quakers were known for their belief in equality and peaceful coexistence. East Jersey, on the other hand, was home to a diverse mix of other Protestant groups. This religious tolerance helped to create a colony that was diverse in its population and beliefs, setting it apart from stricter colonies like Massachusetts.

Relationship with Native Americans

Before European settlers arrived, New Jersey was home to the Lenape, also known as the Delaware people. The Lenni-Lenape named the region Scheyichbi, which means "land bordering the ocean." The arrival of settlers brought significant changes to the lives of the Lenape. While there were initial periods of cooperation and trade, tensions over land ownership and cultural differences led to conflicts, displacing the Lenape from their ancestral lands. In the early years of the colony, some attempts were made to purchase land from the Lenape, but misunderstandings over the nature of land ownership led to disputes.

Government and Politics

In its early years, the colony was governed by the proprietary rule of Carteret and Berkeley, who set up laws and promised settlers freedoms to attract them. The colony's government was based on representative assemblies, where property-owning men could vote for representatives to make laws and decisions. In 1674, under the Treaty of Westminster, London formally gained control of the region. This peace treaty ended the Third Anglo-Dutch War, where England sought to gain dominance over trade routes and colonies that the Dutch controlled.

PARAGRAPH CODE

After reading about **New Jersey**, head back to the reading and number ALL the paragraphs in the reading passage. Then, read each statement below and determine which paragraph **NUMBER** the statement can be found in. Paragraph numbers MAY be used more than one time or not at all. Follow the directions below to reveal the 4-digit code.

A New Jersey's first royal colonial governor was Edward Hyde, also known as Lord Cornbury.

B This region would be named "New Jersey" in honor of Carteret, who had previously served as governor of the Isle of Jersey in England.

C Before European settlers arrived, New Jersey was home to the Lenape, also known as the Delaware people.

D Philip Carteret, appointed by the two proprietors (owners), became the first governor of the proprietary colony.

E The Quakers were known for their belief in equality and peaceful coexistence.

F The "Concession and Agreement" was a document granting religious freedom to all inhabitants of New Jersey.

G New Jersey Colony was founded in 1664 after the English seized the area from the Dutch.

H In exchange for land, settlers in New Jersey were required to pay annual fees called quitrents.

ELIMINATE ALL EVEN-NUMBERED paragraphs that you used as an answer. Record the remaining numbers (in the SAME order in which you recorded them above) in the boxes below.

MYSTERY WORD

After reading about **New Jersey**, determine if each statement below is true or false. Color or shade the boxes of the **TRUE** statements. Next, unscramble the mystery word using the large letters of the **TRUE** statements.

East Jersey's capital was Burlington. **A**	Settlers grew crops such as wheat, corn, barley, oats, and rye. **T**	Philip Carteret, became the first governor of the proprietary colony. **R**	In March of 1673, Sir John Berkeley sold his share of New Jersey. **R**
Scheyichbi, means "land on the hill." **B**	New Jersey Colony was founded in 1687 after the English seized the area from Spain. **C**	Before European settlers arrived, New Jersey was home to the Lenape. **I**	Woodbridge, settled in the fall of 1664, is the oldest township in New Jersey. **E**
Carteret had previously served as governor of the Isle of Jersey in England. **P**	Edward Hyde was also known as Lord Cornbury. **O**	New Jersey welcomed settlers of various faiths. **O**	Under the Treaty of Westminster, London formally gained control of the region. **R**
East Jersey and West Jersey were each governed separately for a time. **S**	The Third Anglo-Dutch War was fought between Mexico and France. **D**	Bergen (present-day Jersey City) was founded in 1660. **P**	In exchange for land, settlers were required to pay annual fees called pesos. **L**

Unscramble the word using the large bold letters of only the **TRUE** statements.

PENNSYLVANIA

Founded in the late 17th century, Pennsylvania was established as a haven for religious freedom. The history of Pennsylvania is closely tied to its founder, William Penn, whose vision of a society based on tolerance and peace shaped the colony's development. Pennsylvania Colony was a proprietary colony until the American Revolution began.

Founding of Pennsylvania

The Pennsylvania Colony was founded in 1681 when King Charles II of England granted a large tract of land to William Penn, a member of the Society of Friends, commonly known as Quakers. The land grant was partly a way for the king to repay a debt owed to Penn's father, Admiral Sir William Penn, and it also served to create a buffer between English colonies and potentially hostile Dutch or Native American territories. Penn named the colony "Pennsylvania," meaning "Penn's Woods," in honor of his father. Sylvania is a Latin word meaning woodland.

A proprietary colony was a type of British colony in North America, where the king granted land to an individual or a group of individuals, known as proprietors (owners). These proprietors were given the authority to govern the land and make decisions about its settlement. However, they were still subject to oversight by the British Crown and had to adhere to English laws.

During the colony's founding, Penn encouraged people to migrate to Pennsylvania by offering attractive land deals. Settlers could purchase land at a rate of forty shillings per one-hundred acres, and larger shares of five-thousand acres were available for one-hundred pounds.

William Penn's Vision

Penn was a Quaker, a religious group that faced persecution in England for their beliefs. Quakers believed in pacifism (conflicts should be resolved peacefully) and equality. Penn's vision for the colony was to create a society without a state church, where individuals could worship freely without interference from the government.

Penn was known for his fair treatment of Native Americans. He sought to establish peaceful relationships with the Indigenous Lenape (Delaware) groups through a series of treaties. He believed that land should be purchased rather than taken, and this policy helped maintain relatively peaceful relations between settlers and Native Americans in the colony's early years.

Economy of the Pennsylvania Colony

The fertile soil and mild climate made the region ideal for farming. Early settlers grew wheat, corn, rye, oats, and barley. Pennsylvania's agricultural surplus was traded locally and exported to other colonies and Europe. The colony also produced lumber from its vast forests, which was used for building ships and homes. The Delaware River served as a key trade route, allowing goods to be easily transported to the port city of Philadelphia, which served as the colonial capital. Philadelphia, founded in 1682, grew into the largest city in the American colonies by the mid-1700s.

Border Disputes

Pennsylvania faced several border disputes in the 1700s with neighboring colonies. Parts of northern Pennsylvania were claimed by both New York and Connecticut, while the southern border was a point of contention with Maryland. Additionally, the southwestern region was claimed by both Pennsylvania and Virginia. Most of these disputes were resolved by 1800. One of the most notable resolutions was the establishment of the Mason-Dixon Line in 1767, surveyed by Charles Mason and Jeremiah Dixon, which set the boundary between Pennsylvania and Maryland.

Government

In 1682, Pennsylvania's first constitution, known as the Frame of Government, was drafted. This document created a bicameral legislature, which consisted of an upper house (Council) and a lower house (General Assembly). The Council was responsible for proposing laws, while the Assembly could either approve or reject them. A year later, the Assembly approved a revised version known as the second Frame of Government.

The Charter of Privileges established a new government in 1701 and replaced the Frame of Government. The Charter simplified the government by eliminating the bicameral legislature. It established a unicameral (single-chamber) legislature, giving the General Assembly more authority to levy (collect) taxes and regulate trade.

Influential Figures

Notable colonists who lived in Pennsylvania included Benjamin Franklin, a Founding Father; Thomas McKean, a signer of the Declaration of Independence; Robert Morris, known as the "Financier of the Revolution;" and Peggy Shippen, the wife of Benedict Arnold.

MYSTERY MATCH

After reading about **Pennsylvania**, draw a line from the left-hand column to make a match in the right-hand column. Your line should go through **ONE** letter. When you complete all the matches, use the letters with a line THROUGH them to unscramble a mystery word. You MUST start and end your line at the **arrow points**.

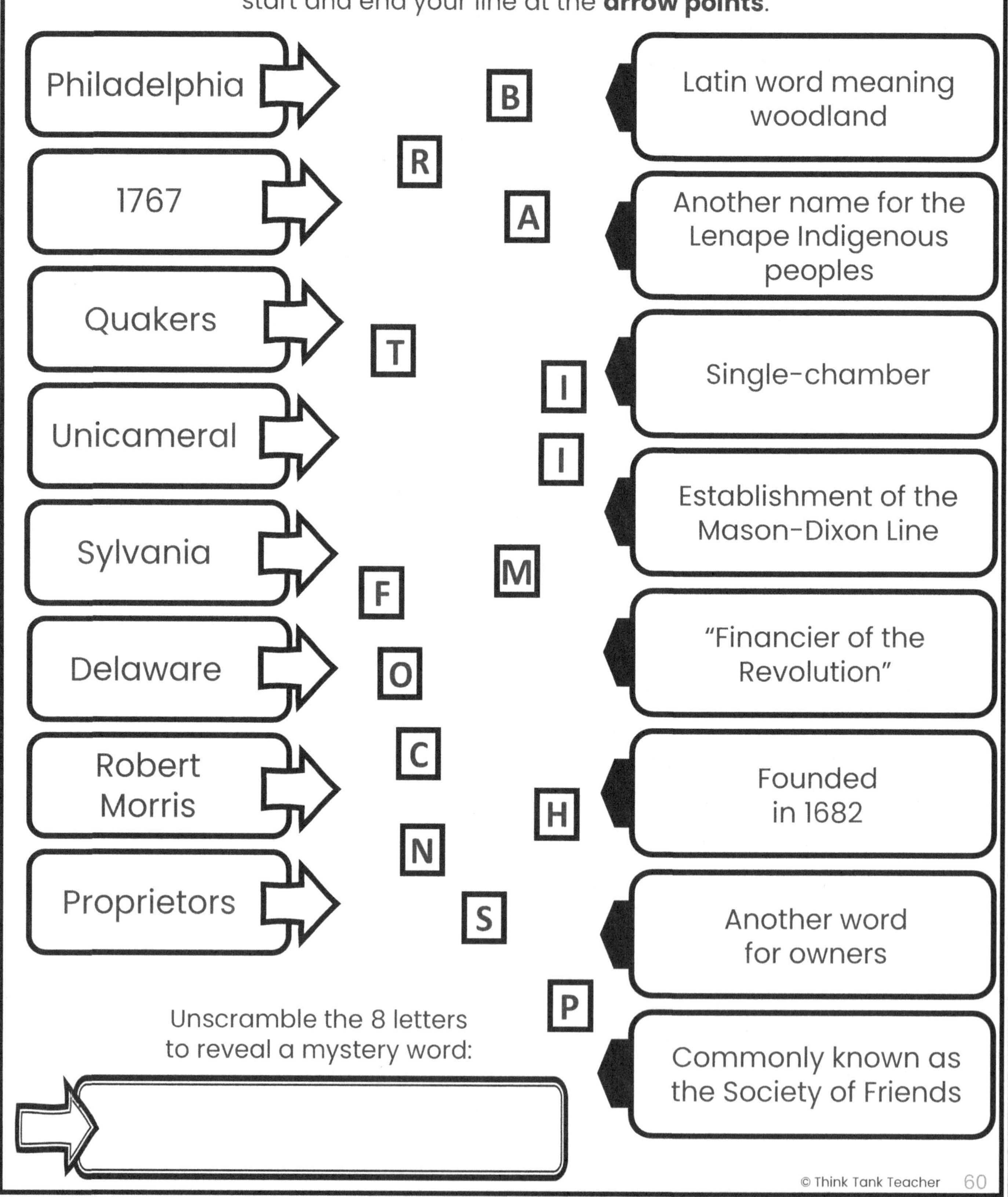

MULTIPLE CHOICE

After reading about **Pennsylvania**, answer each multiple-choice question below. Then, count the number of times you used each letter as an answer (ABCD) to reveal a 4-digit code. Letters may be used more than once or not at all. If a letter option is not used, put a zero in that box.

1 Which city served as the colonial capital of Pennsylvania?

A. Pittsburgh
B. Philadelphia
C. New Haven
D. None of the above

2 What notable colonists lived in Pennsylvania?

A. Thomas McKean
B. Robert Morris
C. Benjamin Franklin
D. All of the above

3 Who granted the large tract of land to William Penn?

A. King Charles II
B. King George II
C. King James II
D. King Andrew II

4 What was Pennsylvania's first constitution known as?

A. Magna Carta
B. Articles of Confederation
C. Frame of Government
D. General Assembly

5 When did the Charter of Privileges replace the Frame of Government?

A. 1682
B. 1683
C. 1697
D. 1701

6 The fertile soil and mild climate made the region ideal for what crops?

A. Rye
B. Barley
C. Wheat
D. All of the above

7 When was the colony of Pennsylvania founded?

A. Late 17th century
B. Early 15th century
C. Late 18th century
D. Mid 14th century

8 What words means "to collect"?

A. Bicameral
B. Levy
C. Propose
D. None of the above

Count how many times you used each letter as a correct answer (ABCD) to determine the 4-digit code. Record your answer in the boxes below.

# of A's	# of B's	# of C's	# of D's

DELAWARE

The Delaware Colony has a history marked by multiple European claims and settlements. The region that is now Delaware was first explored in 1609 by Henry Hudson, who was sailing under the Dutch East India Company. The Dutch were the first to establish a permanent European presence in the area when they settled Zwaanendael (modern-day Lewes) in 1631. However, this settlement was short-lived.

In 1638, the Swedes established the first successful European settlement in Delaware, called Fort Christina (present-day Wilmington), founded by Peter Minuit. This marked the beginning of the colony known as New Sweden. The Swedish presence in the region was relatively peaceful, and they traded with local Native American groups, such as the Lenape and Susquehannock. The name "Delaware" originates from the Delaware River, which was named after Sir Thomas West, the 3rd Baron De La Warr.

Early History

In 1655, the Dutch, under the leadership of Peter Stuyvesant, took control of the Swedish colony, incorporating it into the Dutch territory of New Netherland. Dutch rule did not last long, as the English seized control of the entire region in 1664 during the Second Anglo-Dutch War. This shift in power marked the beginning of English dominance in Delaware, which was granted to James, Duke of York (later King James II).

In 1682, the Duke of York transferred control of Delaware - then known as the "Three Lower Counties" - to William Penn, who was already establishing Pennsylvania as a haven for Quakers. Penn requested the land for a sea route to Pennsylvania. The three counties included New Castle, Sussex, and Kent. New Castle hosted the first assembly meeting, serving as Delaware's colonial capital. Delaware remained under Pennsylvania's administration until 1704 when it formed its own separate assembly, although it continued to share a governor with Pennsylvania until the Revolutionary War.

The Duke's decision angered Charles Calvert, also known as Lord Baltimore, the first proprietary governor of Maryland, who felt entitled to the land in question. This disagreement sparked a lengthy conflict that lasted for a century between the heirs of Penn and those of Baltimore. The dispute was ultimately resolved when the borders of Delaware were clearly defined in 1750. Furthermore, the boundaries between Maryland and Pennsylvania, as well as between Maryland and Delaware, were officially established as part of the Mason-Dixon Line in 1767.

Economy of Delaware Colony

Situated along the Atlantic coast and bordered by the Delaware River, the colony's economy thrived on agriculture, fishing, and trade. The rich soil and moderate climate made it an ideal location for farming crops like rye, wheat, corn, and barley. The Delaware River and its coastline provided opportunities for fishing and shipping. The timber industry also played a significant role in Delaware's economy. The vast forests supplied wood for building ships and constructing homes. In addition, mills were built along the rivers to process grain and timber, further boosting the local economy.

Delaware's early economy also had connections to the labor system of indentured servitude and, later, slavery. Many farms and plantations depended on the labor of enslaved Africans and indentured servants to cultivate crops and work in households.

Religion in the Delaware Colony

Delaware was known for its religious diversity, largely because it passed through the hands of various European powers. The Swedish settlers who established Fort Christina were predominantly Lutheran, bringing their religious practices to the colony. As more settlers arrived, other Protestant groups, such as Presbyterians, Anglicans, and Dutch Reformed Church members, established themselves in the area.

When Delaware came under English control and was administered by William Penn, the colony became a part of his vision of religious tolerance. Penn, a Quaker, sought to create a society where people of different faiths could live together peacefully.

Relations with Native Americans

Delaware's interactions with Native Americans were an important part of its history. Initially, the relationships between the Lenape (Delaware), Susquehannock and European settlers were relatively peaceful and centered on trade.

However, European-introduced diseases, such as smallpox and measles, had a devastating impact on Native American populations in the Delaware Valley, leading to a significant loss of life among the Lenape people.

In addition to the spread of disease, conflicts over land and interactions with the Iroquois Confederacy further pressured the surviving Lenape. As a result, many were forced to relocate from their ancestral lands in search of safety and stability.

TRUE OR FALSE

After reading about **Delaware**, read each statement below and determine if it is true or false. If the statement is true, color the coin that corresponds with that question. If the statement is false, cross out that coin value. When you are finished, add the TOTAL of **ALL TRUE** coin values to reveal a 4-digit code. One digit of the code has been provided for you. If the total is 625, a 6 would go in the first box, the 2 in the second box and so on.

A. In 1682, the Duke of York transferred control of Delaware to William Penn.

B. Delaware remained under Virginia's administration until 1712.

C. European-introduced diseases, such as smallpox and measles, had a devastating impact on Native American populations.

D. The Delaware River and its coastline provided opportunities for fishing and shipping.

E. Charles Calvert was also known as Lord Baltimore.

F. The Three Lower Counties included New Castle, Sussex, and Kent.

G. The region that is now Delaware was first explored in 1609 by Charles Calvert.

H. In 1638, the Swedes established the first successful European settlement in Delaware, called Fort Christina.

After shading the coins based on your answer, add the value of ALL TRUE statements to get the final total. Record your answer in the boxes below.

DOUBLE PUZZLE

After reading about **Delaware**, determine the word that corresponds with the statements provided below. Spell the corresponding word in the boxes to the right. You may or may not use all squares provided for each answer. Any numerical answers must be spelled out. Next, use the numbers **under** indicated letters to reveal a secret word.

1	Swedish settlers established Fort ___						5			
2	The Mason-___ Line was established in 1767					4				
3	Delaware was named after Sir Thomas ___		7							
4	Last name of the first person to explore Delaware in 1609		3							
5	English seized control of the entire region in 1664 during the Second ___-Dutch War					2				
6	New ___ served as the colonial capital of Delaware									
7	Last name of the person also known as Lord Baltimore	1								
8	Penn established Pennsylvania as a haven for ___									
9	___ were built along rivers to process grain and timber		6							
10	Zwaanendael is this modern-day city					8				

SECRET WORD

1	2	3	4	5	6	7	8

SOUTHERN COLONIES

VIRGINIA

The Virginia Colony was the first permanent English settlement in North America. Established in the early 1600s, Virginia became a model for future colonies with its diverse economy, reliance on cash crops, and complex interactions with Native Americans.

Founding of the Virginia Colony

The Virginia Colony was founded in 1607 by the Virginia Company of London, a joint-stock company established by King James I. This company sought to profit from the wealth of the New World. The company sent three ships - Susan Constant, Godspeed, and Discovery - to the New World, arriving near Chesapeake Bay. The settlers established the colony of Jamestown along the James River.

Jamestown faced significant challenges in its early years. Many settlers were unprepared for the harsh conditions, and disease, malnutrition, and conflicts with local Native Americans led to high death rates. Captain John Smith emerged as a key leader during these tough times, helping to organize labor and establish trade relationships with the Powhatan. His efforts were instrumental in keeping the settlement alive.

In 1611, a lieutenant governor named Sir Thomas Dale arrived in Virginia with three-hundred new settlers, soldiers, supplies, and livestock. Dale established strict military codes, inflicting harsh punishment upon lawbreakers. In 1616, Dale sailed back to London to get financial support. That same year, Sir George Yeardley became deputy-governor of Virginia.

The House of Burgesses

In 1619, the colony established the House of Burgesses, the first representative legislative assembly in the New World. This body allowed male property owners to elect representatives who would help make decisions for the colony.

The House of Burgesses was made up of twenty-two burgesses, or representatives. Two delegates from each of the eleven settlements in Virginia, along with a British appointed council and the governor.

The colony, however, remained under the overall authority of the English Crown. In 1624, King James I revoked (canceled) the Virginia Company's charter, making Virginia a royal colony directly under the control of the English monarchy. Despite this change, the House of Burgesses continued to operate.

There were many notable members of the House of Burgesses. George Washington served in the House of Burgesses for 15 years. Patrick Henry was a Patriot who spoke out against the unfair rule of Britain on the colonies. In 1775, the burgesses listened to Patrick Henry deliver his famous "Give me liberty or give me death" speech. Thomas Jefferson represented Albemarle County and served in the House from 1769-1775.

The Economy of Virginia

The economy of the Virginia Colony was initially based on subsistence farming, fishing, and trading with Native Americans. Subsistence farming is when farmers grow crops and raise livestock mainly to feed themselves and their families, rather than for selling or trading.

However, the introduction of tobacco transformed the colony's economic fortunes. In 1612, John Rolfe successfully cultivated a strain of tobacco that was highly popular in England. Tobacco quickly became Virginia's primary cash crop (grown specifically to sell), and its cultivation required large tracts of land and a significant labor force.

To meet the demand for labor, the colony relied on indentured servitude, where people from England worked for a fixed number of years in exchange for passage to the New World. As tobacco plantations expanded, the labor demand grew, leading to the arrival of the first enslaved Africans in 1619.

Religion in Virginia

The Anglican Church (Church of England) was the established church of the colony. Colonists were expected to attend Anglican services and follow its practices. The church played a significant role in the colony's social and political life, with Anglican ministers often serving as community leaders.

Relations with Native Americans

The settlers' arrival in Virginia significantly impacted the region's Indigenous groups, particularly the Powhatan Confederacy, which was a powerful network of Algonquian-speaking populations. Initially, the Powhatan leader, Chief Powhatan, was willing to trade food with the colonists in exchange for European goods. However, as the colonists expanded their settlements and encroached on Native lands, tensions grew.

The relationship between the settlers and the Powhatan deteriorated, leading to a series of violent conflicts known as the Anglo-Powhatan Wars. These wars were marked by brutal fighting and significant losses on both sides. The English emerged victorious, leading to the displacement of many Native Americans.

PARAGRAPH CODE

After reading about **Virginia**, head back to the reading and number ALL the paragraphs in the reading passage. Then, read each statement below and determine which paragraph **NUMBER** the statement can be found in. Paragraph numbers MAY be used more than one time or not at all. Follow the directions below to reveal the 4-digit code.

A The House of Burgesses was made up of twenty-two burgesses, or representatives.

B In 1612, John Rolfe successfully cultivated a strain of tobacco that was highly popular in England.

C This body allowed male property owners to elect representatives who would help make decisions for the colony.

D The Virginia Colony was the first permanent English settlement in North America.

E The church played a significant role in the colony's social and political life, with Anglican ministers often serving as community leaders.

F The company sent three ships - Susan Constant, Godspeed, and Discovery - to the New World, arriving near Chesapeake Bay.

G Subsistence farming is when farmers grow crops and raise livestock mainly to feed themselves and their families.

H The economy of the Virginia Colony was initially based on subsistence farming, fishing, and trading with Native Americans.

ELIMINATE ALL EVEN-NUMBERED paragraphs that you <u>used</u> as an answer. Record the remaining numbers (in the SAME order in which you recorded them above) in the boxes below.

MYSTERY WORD

After reading about **Virginia**, determine if each statement below is true or false. Color or shade the boxes of the **TRUE** statements. Next, unscramble the mystery word using the large letters of the **TRUE** statements.

In 1624, King James I revoked (canceled) the Virginia Company's charter. **L**	In 1775, the burgesses listened to Patrick Henry deliver his famous speech. **A**	The Anglican Church was also known as the Church of England. **S**	In 1597, Sir Thomas Dale arrived in Virginia with nine-hundred new settlers. **N**
The three ships sent to Virginia were the Nina, Pinta, and Santa Maria. **G**	The Virginia Colony was the first permanent English settlement in North America. **B**	Jamestown faced significant challenges in its early years. **Y**	In 1632, the House of Burgesses was established. **O**
Jefferson served in the House of Burgesses from 1769-1775. **S**	The House of Burgesses was made up of thirty-one burgesses. **C**	Cash crops were grown specifically to sell. **M**	In 1618, John Smith successfully cultivated a strain of tobacco. **R**
Jamestown was established along the Mississippi River. **H**	The Powhatan Confederacy was a network of Algonquian-speaking groups. **E**	George Washington served in the House of Burgesses for 27 years. **P**	The Virginia Company of London was established by King George III. **K**

Unscramble the word using the large bold letters of <u>only</u> the **TRUE** statements.

MARYLAND

The Maryland Colony was founded in 1632 when King Charles I of England granted a charter to Cecil Calvert, the second Lord Baltimore. The Calvert family, led by George Calvert, the first Lord Baltimore, had been seeking a place in the New World where Catholics could practice their faith freely, as they faced persecution in Protestant England. When George Calvert died, his son Cecil took over the charter, and Maryland became a refuge for Catholics as well as other religious groups.

Maryland was named Terra Mariae (Mary Land) in honor of Queen Henrietta Maria, the wife of King Charles I. The first settlers, led by Cecil Calvert's brother Leonard Calvert, arrived in 1634 aboard two ships, the Ark and the Dove. They landed at St. Clement's Island in southern Maryland. There, they established the first settlement called St. Mary's City near the mouth of the Potomac River. St. Mary's served as the capital of the colony for many years.

Religion in the Maryland Colony

Although it was intended as a haven for Catholics, Cecil Calvert wanted to create a colony that could accommodate various Christian denominations. In 1649, the colonial assembly passed the Maryland Toleration Act, also known as the Act Concerning Religion. This law guaranteed religious freedom for all Christians, making Maryland one of the first colonies to legislate (pass a law) religious tolerance.

However, the Toleration Act did not extend to non-Christians, and tensions between Catholics and Protestants would occasionally flare up. By the late 1600s, Protestants became the majority in the colony, leading to the repeal (cancel) of the Toleration Act and the establishment of the Church of England as the official religion. Catholics once again faced restrictions, but Maryland remained more religiously diverse than many other colonies.

Economy of the Maryland Colony

The economy of Maryland, like other Southern colonies, was largely agricultural, with a focus on cash crops. The fertile soil and mild climate were ideal for growing tobacco, which quickly became the colony's main export. Tobacco plantations were established along the waterways, and the crop was shipped to Europe in exchange for manufactured goods. Land ownership and the ability to grow cash crops often determined a person's status in the colony.

Tobacco cultivation required large areas of land and significant labor, leading to the use of indentured servants and eventually enslaved Africans. While some indentured servants gained freedom after working for several years, the reliance on enslaved labor increased as the demand for labor grew. By the late 1600s, slavery had become deeply embedded in Maryland's economy and society.

In addition to tobacco, settlers grew corn, wheat, and other grains, and they raised livestock. The colony's location along the Chesapeake Bay and its rivers made fishing, crabbing, and trade important parts of its economy. Baltimore, founded in 1729, would become a major port city, attracting ships from Europe and other colonies.

Government and Social Structure

Maryland began as a proprietary colony, meaning it was governed by the Calvert family rather than directly by the English Crown. Cecil Calvert had significant power as the Lord Proprietor, but he also allowed for the establishment of a colonial assembly, which gave settlers a voice in local government. The colony's government was structured similarly to England's, with a Governor, a Council, and a House of Burgesses. Annapolis was made the capital city in 1695.

Relations with Native Americans

When European settlers arrived in Maryland, they encountered several Algonquian-speaking groups, including the Piscataway and the Susquehannock. Initially, relations were relatively peaceful, with trade between Native Americans and the settlers. However, as the colony expanded, settlers intruded on Native American lands, leading to tensions and occasional conflicts.

Like in many other colonies, European diseases such as smallpox devastated Native American populations, further weakening their ability to resist encroachment (intrusion). Over time, most Native American groups were forced to move away from their traditional lands as European settlement grew.

Challenges and Growth of the Colony

Maryland faced challenges during its early years, including disputes with neighboring colonies, internal religious conflicts, and economic struggles. At times, there were power struggles between the Calvert family and the colonists, who sought more control over their government and laws.

MYSTERY MATCH

After reading about **Maryland**, draw a line from the left-hand column to make a match in the right-hand column. Your line should go through **ONE** letter. When you complete all the matches, use the letters with a line THROUGH them to unscramble a mystery word. You MUST start and end your line at the **arrow points**.

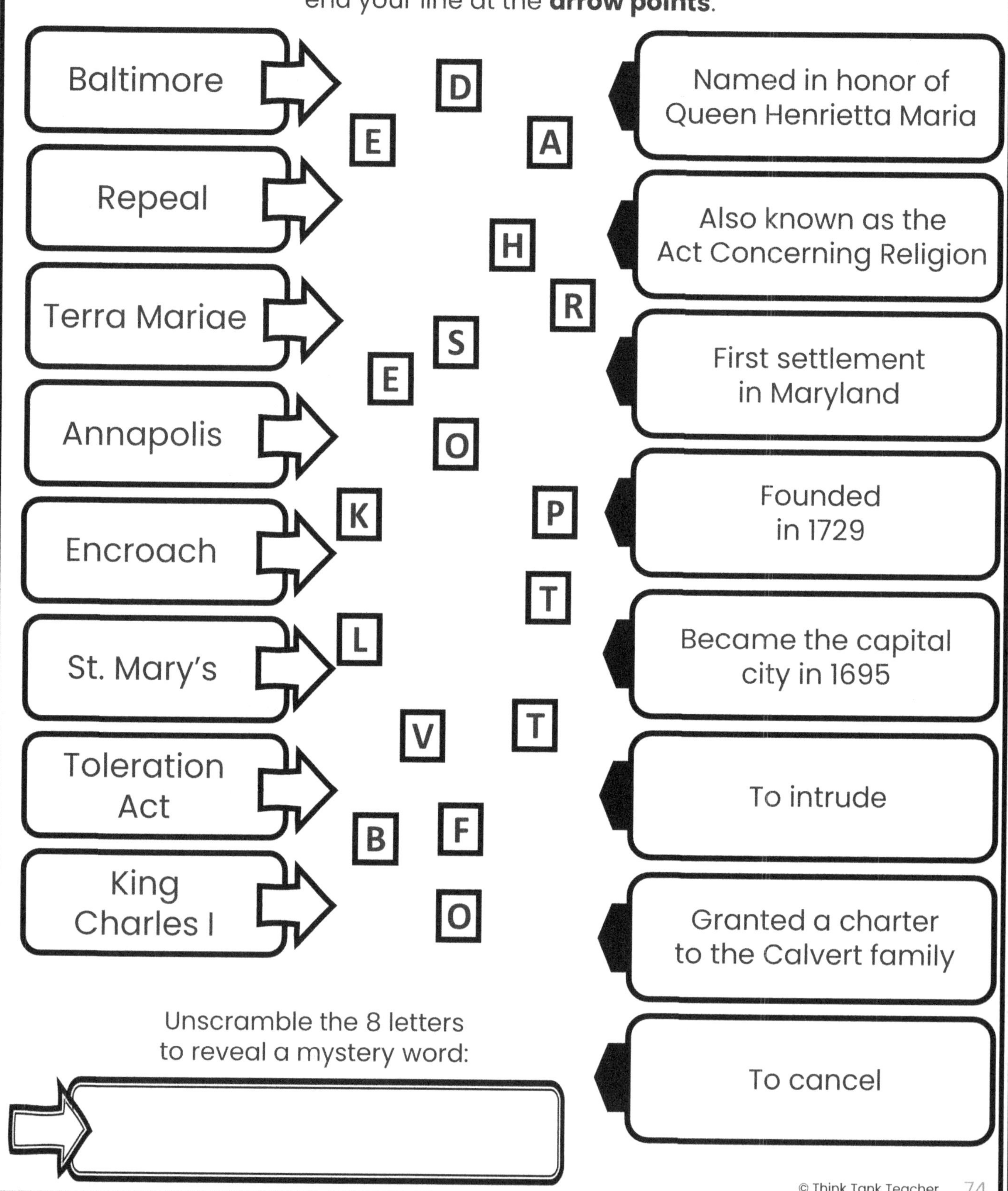

Baltimore
Repeal
Terra Mariae
Annapolis
Encroach
St. Mary's
Toleration Act
King Charles I
D
E
A
H
R
S
E
O
K
P
T
L
V
T
B
F
O
Named in honor of Queen Henrietta Maria
Also known as the Act Concerning Religion
First settlement in Maryland
Founded in 1729
Became the capital city in 1695
To intrude
Granted a charter to the Calvert family
To cancel

Unscramble the 8 letters to reveal a mystery word:

MULTIPLE CHOICE

After reading about **Maryland**, answer each multiple-choice question below. Then, count the number of times you used each letter as an answer (ABCD) to reveal a 4-digit code. Letters may be used more than once or not at all. If a letter option is not used, put a zero in that box.

1 When was the Maryland Toleration Act passed?

A. 1649
B. 1659
C. 1629
D. 1639

2 When European settlers arrived in Maryland, who did they encounter?

A. Piscataway
B. Algonquian-speaking groups
C. Susquehannock
D. All of the above

3 What bay was Maryland located along?

A. Bay of Bengal
B. Chesapeake Bay
C. Apalachee Bay
D. Galveston Bay

4 Who was the wife of King Charles I?

A. Queen Victoria Marie
B. Queen Henrietta Maria
C. Queen Elizabeth III
D. None of the above

5 What challenges did Maryland face in its early years?

A. Disputes with neighboring colonies
B. Internal religious conflicts
C. Economic struggles
D. All of the above

6 What two ships arrived in Maryland in 1634?

A. Discovery and Susan Constant
B. Ark and Dove
C. Mayflower and Speedwell
D. Nina and Pinta

7 Who was known as the first Lord Baltimore?

A. Cecil Calvert
B. George Calvert
C. Leonard Calvert
D. Michael Calvert

8 What does legislate mean?

A. Remove from office
B. Pass a law
C. Intrusion
D. None of the above

Count how many times you used each letter as a correct answer (ABCD) to determine the 4-digit code. Record your answer in the boxes below.

# of A's ______ # of B's ______ # of C's ______ # of D's ______

NORTH CAROLINA

The colony of North Carolina was originally part of the Province of Carolina, which was established in 1663 when King Charles II of England granted a large charter to eight Lord Proprietors. These proprietors (owners) were English nobles who had helped him regain the throne during the English Restoration, and the land was given to them as a reward. The Carolina territory stretched from what is now Virginia to Florida, but over time, North and South Carolina evolved as separate colonies.

Early History

Carolina comes from the Latin word "Carolus," which means Charles. North Carolina's initial settlement dates back to the late 1500s when English explorer Sir Walter Raleigh attempted to establish a colony at Roanoke Island, known as the "Lost Colony." By 1590, all the Roanoke colonists had vanished, and to this day, their fate remains a mystery.

It wasn't until the 1650s that permanent settlers began to arrive, seeking new opportunities for land and resources. These settlers established small farms along the Albemarle Sound and the coastal region. Nathaniel Batts was the first European to permanently settle in North Carolina.

In 1665, Sir John Yeamans attempted to colonize North Carolina along the Cape Fear River (present-day Wilmington). However, the colony struggled, and Yeamans returned to Barbados. The Cape Fear settlement was abandoned in 1667. In 1705, the first permanent town was established in Bath, North Carolina (named after Bath, England).

Economy of the North Carolina Colony

North Carolina's economy benefited from its fertile soil and mild climate. Farmers grew tobacco, corn, wheat, and indigo, but the colony's geography made large-scale plantations difficult. Instead, North Carolina became known for its small family farms rather than vast plantations.

The colony's pine forests were a key economic resource, making North Carolina an important producer of naval stores. These included tar, pitch, and turpentine, which were used for shipbuilding and maintenance. The naval stores industry was crucial to the British Royal Navy, helping to keep ships seaworthy.

Slavery in the North Carolina

Though North Carolina relied on enslaved labor, it did so to a lesser extent compared to other Southern colonies like South Carolina and Virginia. Enslaved Africans were used on tobacco farms and in the production of naval stores, but the smaller farm sizes meant that the population of enslaved people was lower than in other plantation-based economies.

Religion in the North Carolina Colony

Religion in North Carolina was diverse. Many of the early settlers were Anglicans, but Quakers, Presbyterians, Baptists, and Moravians also found a home in the colony. The Quakers were among the first religious groups to establish themselves in North Carolina, especially in the Albemarle region.

Religious tolerance was a key feature of the colony's early years, as there was no strong religious leadership like in Massachusetts. The lack of a dominant church allowed for more freedom of worship, which attracted settlers from various denominations. However, the Anglican Church was eventually established as the official church, with tax support, in the 1700s.

Government and Political Structure

North Carolina started as a proprietary colony, but the region faced difficulties due to poor governance, geographic isolation, and conflicts between settlers and the proprietors. By 1712, North Carolina and South Carolina were officially recognized as separate colonies.

By 1729, after years of unrest and pressure from settlers, North Carolina became a royal colony when the king purchased most of the land rights from the remaining proprietors. John Lord Carteret refused to sell his one-eighth share and later became the Earl of Granville. As a royal colony, it had a royal governor appointed (chosen) by the king and an elected assembly that gave settlers a voice in local government.

Relations with Native Americans

The settlers encountered various Native American groups, including the Tuscarora, Catawba, Cherokee, and Chowanoc. Early interactions often involved trade, but as settlers settled further into Native American territories, tensions escalated.

The Tuscarora, feeling threatened by the expanding European settlements, attacked in 1711. The war lasted for several years and ended with the defeat of the Tuscarora, who eventually migrated northward to join the Iroquois Confederacy. By 1738, about half the Catawba were wiped out by a smallpox epidemic.

TRUE OR FALSE

After reading about **North Carolina**, read each statement below and determine if it is true or false. If the statement is true, color the coin that corresponds with that question. If the statement is false, cross out that coin value. When you are finished, add the TOTAL of **ALL TRUE** coin values to reveal a 4-digit code. One digit of the code has been provided for you. If the total is 625, a 6 would go in the first box, the 2 in the second box and so on.

A. By 1738, about half the Catawba were wiped out by a smallpox epidemic.

B. In 1705, the first permanent town was established in Bath, North Carolina.

C. John Carteret was the first European to permanently settle in North Carolina.

D. North Carolina became known for its small family farms rather than vast plantations.

E. Carolina comes from the Latin word "Carolus," which means cattle.

F. The Cape Fear settlement was abandoned in 1667.

G. King Charles II of England granted a large charter to eight Lord Proprietors.

H. Sir Walter Raleigh attempted to establish a colony at Roanoke Island.

D 100

After shading the coins based on your answer, add the value of ALL TRUE statements to get the final total. Record your answer in the boxes below.

3

DOUBLE PUZZLE

After reading about **North Carolina**, determine the word that corresponds with the statements provided below. Spell the corresponding word in the boxes to the right. You may or may not use all squares provided for each answer. Any numerical answers must be spelled out. Next, use the numbers **under** indicated letters to reveal a secret word.

#	Clue	Boxes (9)	Number under letter
1	First permanent town established in North Carolina		
2	Last name of the proprietor that refused to sell his one-eighth share		3 (under box 3)
3	The Tuscarora migrated northward to join the ___ Confederacy		
4	The ___ Church became the official church in the 1700s		5 (under box 3)
5	Quakers mostly settled in the ___ region		7 (under box 2)
6	Synonym for proprietors		1 (under box 6)
7	Number of proprietors that King Charles I granted charters to		8 (under box 1), 2 (under box 5)
8	Carolina comes from the Latin word "___"		4 (under box 6)
9	Last name of English explorer that attempted to establish Roanoke		6 (under box 6)
10	The Catawba were wiped out by a ___ epidemic		9 (under box 1)

SECRET WORD

1	2	3	4	5	6	7	8	9

SOUTH CAROLINA

South Carolina was officially founded in 1670 as a proprietary colony, initially part of the larger Province of Carolina. This land was granted to eight Lords Proprietors by King Charles II of England. The Lords Proprietors included notable figures such as Anthony Ashley Cooper, the 1st Earl of Shaftesbury, Sir George Carteret, and Sir John Colleton.

Before Europeans arrived in South Carolina, the region was home to several Indigenous groups, with the Catawba and Cherokee being the most prominent. The Cherokee lived in the western part of the region, near the Blue Ridge Mountains. The Catawba settled in the northern region, around Rock Hill.

Permanent Settlement

The first permanent settlement, known as Charles Town (present-day Charleston), was established in 1670 near the merging of the Ashley and Cooper Rivers. The site was strategically chosen for its natural harbor, making it ideal for trade and commerce.

Among the key figures in the early establishment of the colony was Sir John Yeamans, who served as governor from 1672 to 1674. His leadership was instrumental in shaping the early governance of the colony.

The settlement quickly grew, becoming a melting pot of cultures, including English, French Huguenots, and Spanish settlers. The settlement attracted a diverse group of colonists, including planters, tradespeople, and merchants.

As the population grew, so did the need for infrastructure. Settlers built homes, shops, and public buildings, turning Charles Town into a thriving community. By the late 17th century, it had become the principal seat of government for the entire region.

By 1712, North Carolina and South Carolina were officially recognized as separate colonies due to differences in geography, population, and governance, marking the formal split between the two regions.

Economy

The economy of South Carolina was predominantly agrarian (farming), characterized by the cultivation of cash crops. The primary crops were rice and indigo, which became highly lucrative (profitable) in European markets. Rice cultivation, in particular, thrived in the lowland areas of the colony, where the marshy landscape was ideal for irrigation.

By the late 17th century, rice had become the backbone of the South Carolina economy. Wealthy planters, such as Henry Laurens and John Rutledge, owned large plantations and developed irrigation systems to maximize rice production. The labor-intensive nature of rice farming led to a significant increase in the importation of enslaved Africans. By the early 18th century, enslaved individuals made up the majority of the population.

Religion

While the Church of England served as the established church, the colony attracted a variety of religious groups. French Huguenots, fleeing persecution in France, brought Calvinist beliefs, while Quakers and other dissenting sects (groups) added to the diversity of religious tolerance.

Notable religious figures included William Henry Drayton, a prominent Anglican, and George Whitefield, a preacher who helped spread the Great Awakening movement in the colonies.

Governance

Initially ruled by the Lords Proprietors, South Carolina underwent significant changes in governance. In 1729, it transitioned to a royal colony under direct control of the British Crown, resulting in a more structured government with a governor, a council, and a legislative assembly. The first royal governor was Robert Johnson, who served from 1735 to 1738.

Johnson's "Township Scheme" aimed to create frontier settlements that would act as a protective buffer between the coastal areas and potential threats from Native Americans, as well as Spanish and French forces. Under Johnson's plan, the government offered significant land grants to attract individuals and families willing to cultivate the land and establish communities. Other incentives included reduced taxes and exemptions from certain duties for a specified period.

Conflict and Development

As South Carolina expanded, it encountered conflicts with Native Americans, particularly the Cherokee and Yamasee. Encroachment (intrusion) on Native lands and unfair trade practices led to the Yamasee War in 1715. Initially, the Yamasee and their allies achieved several victories, but the English settlers quickly regrouped and launched a counteroffensive. By 1717, the conflict had largely ended, with many Yamasee fleeing to Spanish Florida. This conflict temporarily destabilized (weakened) the colony, resulting in the loss of lives on both sides.

PARAGRAPH CODE

After reading about **South Carolina**, head back to the reading and number ALL the paragraphs in the reading passage. Then, read each statement below and determine which paragraph **NUMBER** the statement can be found in. Paragraph numbers MAY be used more than one time or not at all. Follow the directions below to reveal the 4-digit code.

A The settlement quickly grew, becoming a melting pot of cultures, including English, French Huguenots, and Spanish settlers.

B Encroachment (intrusion) on Native lands and unfair trade practices led to the Yamasee War in 1715.

C The Cherokee lived in the western part of the region, near the Blue Ridge Mountains.

D The labor-intensive nature of rice farming led to a significant increase in the importation of enslaved Africans.

E The economy of South Carolina was predominantly agrarian (farming), characterized by the cultivation of cash crops.

F The first royal governor was Robert Johnson, who served from 1735 to 1738.

G South Carolina was officially founded in 1670 as a proprietary colony, initially part of the larger Province of Carolina.

H By the late 17th century, rice had become the backbone of the South Carolina economy.

ELIMINATE ALL EVEN-NUMBERED paragraphs that you <u>used</u> as an answer. Record the remaining numbers (in the SAME order in which you recorded them above) in the boxes below.

MYSTERY WORD

After reading about **South Carolina**, determine if each statement below is true or false. Color or shade the boxes of the **TRUE** statements. Next, unscramble the mystery word using the large letters of the **TRUE** statements.

Charles Town was established at the merging of the Potomac and Missouri Rivers. **H**	The first royal governor was Robert Johnson, who served from 1735 to 1738. **L**	French Huguenots, fleeing persecution, brought Calvinist beliefs. **A**	South Carolina did not support religious diversity or religious tolerance. **K**
In 1729, South Carolina transitioned to a royal colony. **T**	Anthony Ashley Cooper was the 1st Earl of Shaftesbury. **I**	King Charles II granted land in the Carolinas to thirteen proprietors. **B**	The Yamasee War began in 1737. **O**
The Catawba settled in the northern region, around Rock Hill. **E**	South Carolina was initially part of the larger Province of Carolina. **U**	The economy of South Carolina was predominantly hunting and fishing. **R**	By the late 17th century, rice had become the backbone of the South Carolina economy. **V**
George Whitefield, a preacher, helped spread the Great Awakening movement. **C**	By 1607, North Carolina and South Carolina were officially recognized as separate colonies. **N**	The first permanent settlement of South Carolina was known as Colleton. **D**	Sir John Yeamans served as governor from 1672 to 1674. **T**

Unscramble the word using the large bold letters of only the **TRUE** statements.

GEORGIA

The Georgia Colony, the last of the original thirteen colonies, was founded in 1732 and settled in 1733. It was established by James Oglethorpe, a member of Parliament, social reformer, and military leader. Oglethorpe's vision for Georgia was unique: he sought to create a place where England's poor and indebted could start anew, while also establishing a strategic buffer zone between the British colonies and Spanish-controlled Florida.

King George II granted Oglethorpe and a group of trustees a charter for the land between the Savannah and Altamaha Rivers on June 9, 1732. The colony was named "Georgia" in honor of King George II. Oglethorpe, along with the first group of 120 settlers, arrived on the ship *Anne* and landed in what would become Savannah in February of 1733. The city of Savannah (formerly known as Yamacraw Bluff), became Georgia's first settlement and capital.

Settlement and Governance

Georgia was intended to serve as a refuge for debtors - people who were imprisoned in England because they could not pay their debts. Oglethorpe was troubled by the harsh conditions faced by those in debtors' prisons, and he believed that they deserved a second chance to rebuild their lives.

Oglethorpe's plan was to offer the debtors a fresh start in the New World, where they could work, farm, and contribute to the economy of the new colony. While this vision was initially a key part of the founding of Georgia, in reality, not many debtors were actually sent there. Instead, many settlers who came to Georgia were poor English citizens looking for a new start.

Oglethorpe and the trustees wanted Georgia to serve as a colony with no slavery, no large estates, and no rum (alcohol). They created regulations to ensure that each settler received an equal amount of land, prohibiting large landholdings to prevent economic inequality. Additionally, slavery was initially banned to promote a community of small farms and to prevent wealthy landowners from having all the power. Religious freedom was another cornerstone, welcoming groups like persecuted Protestants, including the Salzburgers from Austria and the Moravians from Central Europe. Oglethorpe served as the colonial governor of Georgia for 12 years.

Economy of the Georgia Colony

Initially, Georgia's economy was intended to revolve around small-scale agriculture, with a focus on crops like silk, wine, and olives, which the trustees believed would thrive in the warm climate. However, these efforts were mostly unsuccessful, and settlers began to turn to other crops better suited to the region, such as rice, indigo, and tobacco.

The restrictions on landownership and slavery created economic challenges, as many settlers struggled to compete with the more prosperous plantation economies of neighboring South Carolina. By 1750, after Oglethorpe returned to England, the trustees lifted the ban on slavery, allowing Georgia's economy to shift towards plantation agriculture. This led to the rapid growth of rice and indigo plantations, which were labor-intensive and required enslaved African laborers. In 1752, frustrated by the lack of economic success, the trustees returned control of Georgia to the British Crown, making it a royal colony.

Religion in Georgia

While Georgia was founded with a degree of religious freedom, it was still influenced by the Anglican Church, the official church of England. The Church of England was established in the colony, and Anglican ministers were sent to spread their teachings. However, Georgia was also known for being a refuge for those facing religious persecution in Europe.

A notable religious group in the early days of the colony was the Salzburgers, German-speaking Protestants who had been expelled (forced to leave) from their home in present-day Austria because of their faith. They established a settlement called Ebenezer in 1734, northeast of Savannah. Johann Martin Boltzius served as the minister to the Salzburger community at Ebenezer for three decades. His leadership was instrumental in ensuring the community's growth and success during this time.

Other groups like Scottish Highlanders, Jews, and Methodists also made their homes in Georgia. The Jewish settlers, who arrived in Savannah in 1733, included Dr. Samuel Nunes, who became the colony's first physician. These settlers made significant contributions to the colony's culture and diversity, even though some initial resistance to their presence existed.

Challenges and Conflicts

Oglethorpe's role as both a military leader and a governor put him at the forefront of defending the colony from Spanish attacks. In 1742, he led the defense of Georgia during the Battle of Bloody Marsh on St. Simons Island, where British and colonial forces successfully repelled a Spanish invasion from Florida. This victory solidified Georgia's position as a crucial buffer between the British colonies and Spanish Florida.

MYSTERY MATCH

After reading about **Georgia**, draw a line from the left-hand column to make a match in the right-hand column. Your line should go through **ONE** letter. When you complete all the matches, use the letters with a line THROUGH them to unscramble a mystery word. You MUST start and end your line at the **arrow points**.

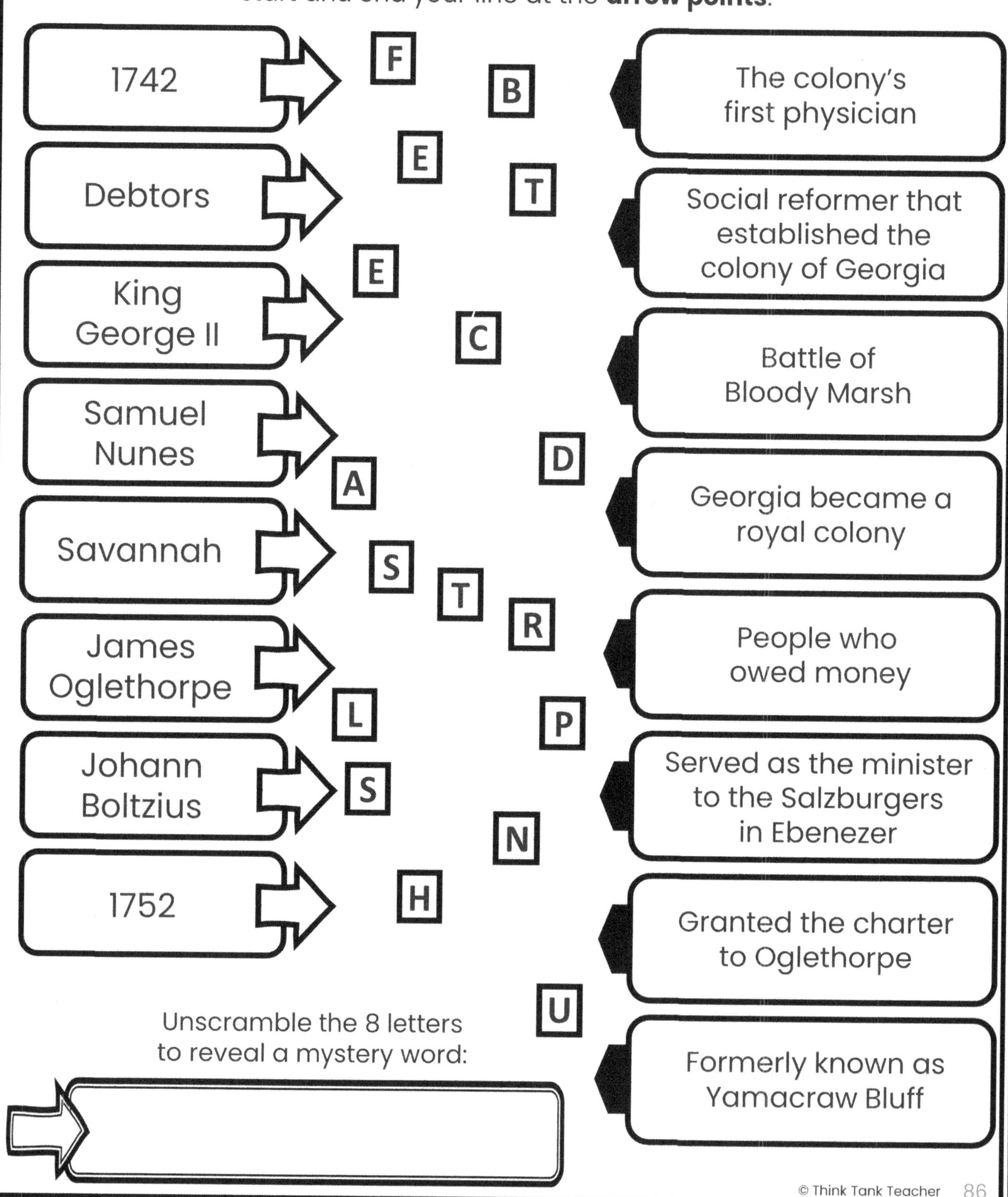

1742
Debtors
King George II
Samuel Nunes
Savannah
James Oglethorpe
Johann Boltzius
1752
F
B
E
T
E
C
D
A
S
T
R
L
P
S
N
H
U
The colony's first physician
Social reformer that established the colony of Georgia
Battle of Bloody Marsh
Georgia became a royal colony
People who owed money
Served as the minister to the Salzburgers in Ebenezer
Granted the charter to Oglethorpe
Formerly known as Yamacraw Bluff
Unscramble the 8 letters to reveal a mystery word:

MULTIPLE CHOICE

After reading about **Georgia**, answer each multiple-choice question below. Then, count the number of times you used each letter as an answer (ABCD) to reveal a 4-digit code. Letters may be used more than once or not at all. If a letter option is not used, put a zero in that box.

1 Oglethorpe was granted a charter for land between what two rivers?

A. Ohio and Potomac Rivers
B. Missouri and Rio Grande Rivers
C. Mississippi and St. Johns Rivers
D. Savannah and Altamaha Rivers

2 Where were the Salzburgers originally from?

A. Norway
B. Russia
C. Spain
D. Austria

3 What city became Georgia's first settlement and capital?

A. Atlanta
B. Macon
C. Abbeville
D. Savannah

4 Oglethorpe, along with the first group of 120 settlers, arrived on what ship?

A. George
B. Anne
C. Nunes
D. None of the above

5 How many years did Oglethorpe serve as Georgia's governor?

A. 4 years
B. 8 years
C. 12 years
D. 16 years

6 The Battle of Bloody Marsh was fought between the British and who?

A. French Canada
B. French Louisiana
C. Spanish Florida
D. Spanish Texas

7 What groups made Georgia their home?

A. Scottish Highlanders
B. Methodists
C. Salzburgers
D. All of the above

8 What does the word "expelled" mean?

A. Money owed
B. Approved or enacted
C. Forced to leave
D. Small farms

Count how many times you used each letter as a correct answer (ABCD) to determine the 4-digit code. Record your answer in the boxes below.

# of A's	# of B's	# of C's	# of D's

JAMESTOWN

The founding of Jamestown in 1607 marked the beginning of the first permanent English settlement in North America. Sponsored by the Virginia Company of London, a joint-stock company chartered by King James I, the settlement was established with the hopes of finding riches, and to establish a foothold for England in the New World.

The Virginia Company was backed by private investors who expected a return on their investment. They expected to find gold in the New World. They were also eager to find a river route to the Pacific Ocean so that they could establish trade with Asia.

Journey to the New World

The charter brought together a large group of men and on December 20, 1606, they set sail in three ships called the Susan Constant, Godspeed, and the Discovery. The expedition to the New World included one hundred forty-four men. After traveling across the Atlantic Ocean for four months, and stopping in Puerto Rico for food and water, they landed in Virginia on April 26, 1607. The Discovery, the smallest ship, was later used in attempts to find the legendary Northwest Passage.

The colonists selected a location roughly forty miles up the James River, which they named in honor of King James I. They believed this spot was advantageous for defense, as it was far enough inland to avoid Spanish ships and offered a good deep-water port. The river would also serve as a key transportation route. Jamestown was established in the middle of the Paspahegh territory, a tributary of the Powhatan.

The settlers were mostly businessmen who did not know how to hunt, fish or farm. In the long run, the site later proved to be a disaster. The men arrived in late summer and were unable to plant crops to have food to eat. They relied heavily on supplies from England that took months to arrive.

The Early Struggles

In summer months, the land turned into swampy, poisonous waters full of disease-ridden mosquitos and unhealthy drinking water. Malaria, dysentery, and typhoid fever plagued the settlement, causing widespread illness and death. The settlers' lack of immunity to the new environment made them vulnerable to these diseases. In the winter, they had no protection against the bitter cold.

In 1608, Captain John Smith took over as the president of the colony. He was a highly experienced soldier and seaman. Because of Smith, the settlers were able to survive and feed themselves. He required everyone to work, which made many settlers dislike him. He enforced a new rule that stated, “If you don’t work, you don’t eat."

Relations with the Powhatan

Relations with the Powhatan Confederacy were complex and often tense. While there were instances of trade and diplomacy, there were also conflicts over land and resources. A notable story from this period involves the interaction between John Smith and Pocahontas, the daughter of Chief Powhatan. According to Smith’s account, Pocahontas saved his life when her father threatened to kill him.

After Pocahontas stepped in to make sure Smith was not harmed, the Natives and the settlers were able to get along and trade goods that the settlers needed. Settlers gave the Powhatan tools, pots, and knives in exchange for food such as corn.

The colony fell to chaos between 1609 and 1610 when John Smith was injured by a gunpowder explosion. George Percy then became the leader of the colony. Percy was unable to keep good relationships with the Powhatan. That year was known as the “Starving Time.”

After Smith was injured and had to return to England, the colonists had to survive the harshest winter yet. Several supply ships became lost or wrecked so colonists began boiling and eating shoe leather and rats. Of the five hundred settlers, only about sixty remained. Eventually, a ship with supplies arrived from England.

By 1610, new conflicts between colonists and Natives started the first of three Anglo-Powhatan Wars. During the Powhatan Wars, Pocahontas was captured and held hostage by the British.

Jamestown served as capital of the colony of Virginia for more than eighty years. Initially, the colony was more of a failure than a success. But in 1612, a colonist named John Rolfe began growing tobacco. Tobacco quickly became the colony's first profitable export, transforming Jamestown’s economy.

In 1614, Rolfe's marriage to Pocahontas helped bring a period of relative peace between the English settlers and the Powhatan Confederacy, known as the "Peace of Pocahontas." However, this peace was temporary, and tensions eventually resurfaced, leading to further conflicts. In 1624, King James I revoked the Virginia Company’s charter, making Virginia a royal colony under direct control of the English crown.

TRUE OR FALSE

After reading about **Jamestown**, read each statement below and determine if it is true or false. If the statement is true, color the coin that corresponds with that question. If the statement is false, cross out that coin value. When you are finished, add the TOTAL of **ALL TRUE** coin values to reveal a 4-digit code. One digit of the code has been provided for you. If the total is 625, a 6 would go in the first box, the 2 in the second box and so on.

A. Jamestown was established in the middle of the Paspahegh territory, a tributary of the Powhatan.

B. In 1616, King George II I revoked the Virginia Company's charter.

C. The colony fell to chaos between 1609 and 1610 when John Smith was injured by a gunpowder explosion.

D. The expedition to the New World included seven hundred twenty-one men.

E. The Santa Maria, the smallest ship, was later used in attempts to find the legendary Northwest Passage.

F. Jamestown served as capital of the colony for more than two hundred years.

G. Settlers gave the Powhatan tools, pots, and knives in exchange for food such as corn.

H. The founding of Jamestown in 1617 marked the beginning of the first permanent French settlement in North America.

After shading the coins based on your answer, add the value of ALL TRUE statements to get the final total. Record your answer in the boxes below.

DOUBLE PUZZLE

After reading about **Jamestown**, determine the word that corresponds with the statements provided below. Spell the corresponding word in the boxes to the right. You may or may not use all squares provided for each answer. Any numerical answers must be spelled out. Next, use the numbers **under** indicated letters to reveal a secret word.

#	Statement	Boxes (9)	Number under box
1	Number of ships the group set sail on in December of 1606	☐☐☐☐☐☐☐☐☐	4 (box 2)
2	Last name of man that introduced tobacco	☐☐☐☐☐☐☐☐☐	
3	"If you don't work, you don't ___"	☐☐☐☐☐☐☐☐☐	5 (box 2)
4	Jamestown was the first permanent ___ settlement in North America	☐☐☐☐☐☐☐☐☐	8 (box 2)
5	1609-1610 was known as the "___ Time"	☐☐☐☐☐☐☐☐☐	6 (box 2)
6	The Discovery was used to find the legendary ___ Passage	☐☐☐☐☐☐☐☐☐	3 (box 6)
7	The Virginia Company was backed by ___ investors	☐☐☐☐☐☐☐☐☐	7 (box 5)
8	Last name of Jamestown's leader after John Smith	☐☐☐☐☐☐☐☐☐	1 (box 1)
9	The Virginia Company of London was a joint-___ company	☐☐☐☐☐☐☐☐☐	2 (box 3)
10	Colonists selected a location roughly forty miles up this river	☐☐☐☐☐☐☐☐☐	

SECRET WORD

☐	☐	☐	☐	☐	☐	☐	☐
1	2	3	4	5	6	7	8

ROANOKE

Roanoke Colony was England's first attempt to establish a new colony in the Americas. The story of the Lost Colony of Roanoke is one of the oldest mysteries in American history. Established in the late 16th century on Roanoke Island, off the coast of present-day North Carolina, the colony disappeared under mysterious circumstances, leaving behind little evidence of what happened to its settlers. The colony is often referred to as the "Lost Colony."

In 1584, Queen Elizabeth I granted the land of Virginia to Sir Walter Raleigh. England wanted to establish a colony as an attempt to expand the British Empire in the New World. This charter specifically stated that Raleigh must establish a North American colony, or he would lose his right to colonization. Raleigh's goal was to establish a base that could be used for trade and as a strategic location for attacking Spanish ships.

Raleigh sent Captain Amada and Captain Barlowe to explore the new area. The explorers reached Roanoke Island off the coast of North Carolina on July 4th, 1584. At that time, the land was considered a part of Virginia. The men mapped the area, decided it would be a good area to colonize and then returned to England.

Attempts to Settle

Sir Richard Greenville led the first expedition to Roanoke Island in 1585. The expedition arrived at Roanoke about one year after Amada and Barlowe looked for places to settle a colony. In Roanoke, Greenville left his male settlers under the charge of Ralph Lane. Greenville returned to England to gather supplies for the settlement.

The settlers built a fort and explored the surrounding areas. However, the colony faced difficulties almost immediately. They struggled with food shortages and conflicts with local Native American groups, such as the Algonquian-speaking people led by Chief Wingina, also known as Pemisapan. During their exploration of the coast, the Europeans blamed the locals for stealing a silver cup. As revenge, the settlers burned their village ruining relations with Native Americans.

The supplies did not arrive as planned, so many of the colonists headed back to England with Sir Francis Drake. Eventually, Greenville returned to Roanoke Island but found that it was deserted (left empty). Greenville left some men on the island once again and returned to England a second time for supplies.

In 1587, a group of settlers led by John White arrived at Roanoke. There were ninety men, thirteen women, and eleven children. Upon arrival they found the skeletal remains of Greenville's men. These settlers decided to stay and build a new life and new home for their families.

John White's Departure

Building a new settlement was a struggle and disputes with the local Native Americans forced John White to return to England for more supplies. The colonists realized they were not prepared to build a successful colony. While White was gone his granddaughter was born on Roanoke Island. Virginia Dare was the first child born in the Americas to English parents.

In England, White found little help for his colony because England was battling with Spain in the Anglo-Spanish War. Due to the Spanish Armada, White was not able to return to Roanoke for three years. Every English ship joined the fight, leaving White with no way of returning to Roanoke.

When White was finally able to return to Roanoke, he found the colony was completely abandoned. There were no signs of struggle. White assumed the colonists had moved to a nearby island called Croatoan. However, White's search was cut short due to severe weather prevented and forced his return to England.

The only clue left behind was the word "Croatoan" carved into a gatepost and "Cro" carved into a tree. White believed that "Croatoan" referred to Croatoan Island (now known as Hatteras Island), where the friendly Croatoans lived. No one ever heard from or saw the colonists again.

Theories About the Disappearance

The disappearance of the Roanoke settlers has sparked numerous theories over the centuries. Some historians believe that the settlers may have integrated with local Native Americans to survive.

Another possibility is that the settlers attempted to relocate inland, where they could have faced challenges such as disease, lack of food, or attacks from hostile Natives. Other theories include the possibility of Spanish attacks on the settlement. No definitive evidence has ever been found.

Today, the area is called Dare County, North Carolina. The site of the original Roanoke settlement is now part of the Fort Raleigh National Historic Site on Roanoke Island. Visitors can explore the area, learn about the history of the attempts to establish the first English colony in America, and reflect on the long-term mystery of the Lost Colony.

PARAGRAPH CODE

After reading about **Roanoke**, head back to the reading and number ALL the paragraphs in the reading passage. Then, read each statement below and determine which paragraph **NUMBER** the statement can be found in. Paragraph numbers MAY be used more than one time or not at all. Follow the directions below to reveal the 4-digit code.

A The disappearance of the Roanoke settlers has sparked numerous theories over the centuries.

B The expedition arrived at Roanoke about one year after Amada and Barlowe looked for places to settle a colony.

C Due to the Spanish Armada, White was not able to return to Roanoke for three years.

D The story of the Lost Colony of Roanoke is one of the oldest mysteries in American history.

E The site of the original Roanoke settlement is now part of the Fort Raleigh National Historic Site.

F There were ninety men, thirteen women, and eleven children.

G England wanted to establish a colony as an attempt to expand the British Empire in the New World.

H Raleigh sent Captain Amada and Captain Barlowe to explore the new area.

ELIMINATE ALL EVEN-NUMBERED paragraphs that you used as an answer. Record the remaining numbers (in the SAME order in which you recorded them above) in the boxes below.

MYSTERY WORD

After reading about **Roanoke**, determine if each statement below is true or false. Color or shade the boxes of the **TRUE** statements. Next, unscramble the mystery word using the large letters of the **TRUE** statements.

In Roanoke, Greenville left his male settlers under the charge of Ralph Lane. **D**	At the time, England was battling with Spain in the Anglo-Spanish War. **E**	Roanoke was established in the late 19th century. **A**	In 1591, a group of settlers led by John Rolfe arrived at Roanoke. **C**
Sir Richard Greenville led the first expedition to Roanoke Island in 1585. **N**	Roanoke Island is off the coast of present-day Pennsylvania. **L**	Today, the area is called Dare County, North Carolina. **E**	When White returned to Roanoke, he found signs of struggle and stress. **G**
Virginia Dare was the first child born in the Americas to English parents. **C**	Raleigh sent Captain Adrian and Captain Bentley to explore the new area. **H**	Due to the Spanish Armada, White couldn't return to Roanoke for three years. **I**	The supplies to Roanoke arrived as planned, in a timely manner. **R**
Croatoan Island is now known as Cape Canaveral. **T**	Chief Wingina was also known as Squanto. **P**	At Roanoke, Europeans blamed the locals for stealing a silver cup. **E**	In 1584, Queen Elizabeth I granted the land of Virginia to Sir Walter Raleigh. **V**

Unscramble the word using the large bold letters of <u>only</u> the **TRUE** statements.

POCAHONTAS

Pocahontas, a Native American woman of the Powhatan Confederacy, holds a significant place in American history as a figure who served as a bridge between Native Americans and English settlers. Born around 1596 in what is now Virginia, she was originally named Amonute, with the more familiar name Pocahontas serving as a childhood nickname, meaning "playful one" or "little mischief." Her father, Chief Powhatan, was the leader of the Powhatan Confederacy, a powerful alliance of thirty Native American nations, that dominated the Tidewater region of Virginia.

Early Encounters with the English

Pocahontas first became known to the English settlers in 1607, the year the Jamestown colony was founded. The English, led by Captain John Smith, established the first permanent English settlement in North America.

According to a famous story told by John Smith, Pocahontas saved his life after he was captured by the Powhatan. He claimed that as he was about to be harmed, Pocahontas rushed to Smith's side and intervened. Historians debate the accuracy of this story, as it was written years after the event. While Smith's story has become a well-known part of American folklore, many historians view it with skepticism. They believe it may be an exaggerated or misinterpreted account rather than a literal rescue.

Despite the questions surrounding this event, it is clear that Pocahontas played a key role in the early interactions between the English settlers and the Powhatan people. She frequently visited the Jamestown colony, bringing food to help the struggling settlers survive their first difficult winters. Her presence and assistance helped maintain a fragile peace between the two groups during the colony's early years. Pocahontas was around age ten when the colonists arrived in Virginia.

In 1609, John Smith was injured in a gunpowder accident and returned to England to receive medical treatment. Colonists told Pocahontas that John Smith died. As a result, she stopped visiting the colony for several years.

Tensions Rise

In 1613, Pocahontas was captured by English Captain Samuel Argall during a conflict between the settlers and her people. She was held for ransom, with the English demanding that Chief Powhatan release English prisoners and return stolen weapons in exchange for her freedom. While in captivity, Pocahontas was treated well and converted to Christianity, taking the name Rebecca. She was taught about Christianity by Reverend Alexander Whitaker. During her captivity, she met John Rolfe, an English tobacco planter.

Marriage to John Rolfe and Journey to England

In 1614, Pocahontas married John Rolfe, a union that brought a temporary period of peace between the English settlers and the Powhatan Confederacy, known as the "Peace of Pocahontas." This period of peace lasted eight years. The marriage helped solidify relations between the two groups, and it also had significant economic implications. Rolfe was instrumental in the development of tobacco as a cash crop in Virginia, which became a critical element of the colony's economy.

In 1616, Pocahontas traveled to England with her husband and their son, Thomas Rolfe. The Virginia Company, which had funded the Jamestown settlement, used her trip to gain support for the colony. Pocahontas was presented to English society as a symbol of the "civilized" Native American and met with various dignitaries (notable leaders), including King James I. Her visit to England was intended to demonstrate the potential for positive relationships between the English and Native Americans.

Final Days and Legacy

While in England, Pocahontas became ill, possibly from smallpox, pneumonia, tuberculosis, or another European disease. As the Rolfe family prepared to return to Virginia, Pocahontas' health worsened, and she died in March 1617 in Gravesend, England, at about 21 years old. She was buried at St. George's Church in Gravesend.

After Pocahontas' death, John Rolfe wanted to resume his voyage to Virginia with his two-year-old son. Sadly, the boy was ill, so Rolfe left him with Sir Lewis Stukely in Plymouth, England. John Rolfe never saw his son again. Rolfe's brother, Henry, eventually took care of Thomas.

Pocahontas' gravesite beneath the church at Gravesend was destroyed by a fire in 1727. A bronze statue, sculpted by William Ordway Partridge, was placed on Jamestown Island in 1907 for the 300th anniversary of the settlement. A statue in England was dedicated in 1958 as a replica of Jamestown's statue. Today, Pocahontas is remembered not just as a historical figure, but as a symbol of cultural exchange and the challenges faced by Native Americans during the colonization of North America.

MYSTERY MATCH

After reading about **Pocahontas**, draw a line from the left-hand column to make a match in the right-hand column. Your line should go through **ONE** letter. When you complete all the matches, use the letters with a line THROUGH them to unscramble a mystery word. You MUST start and end your line at the **arrow points**.

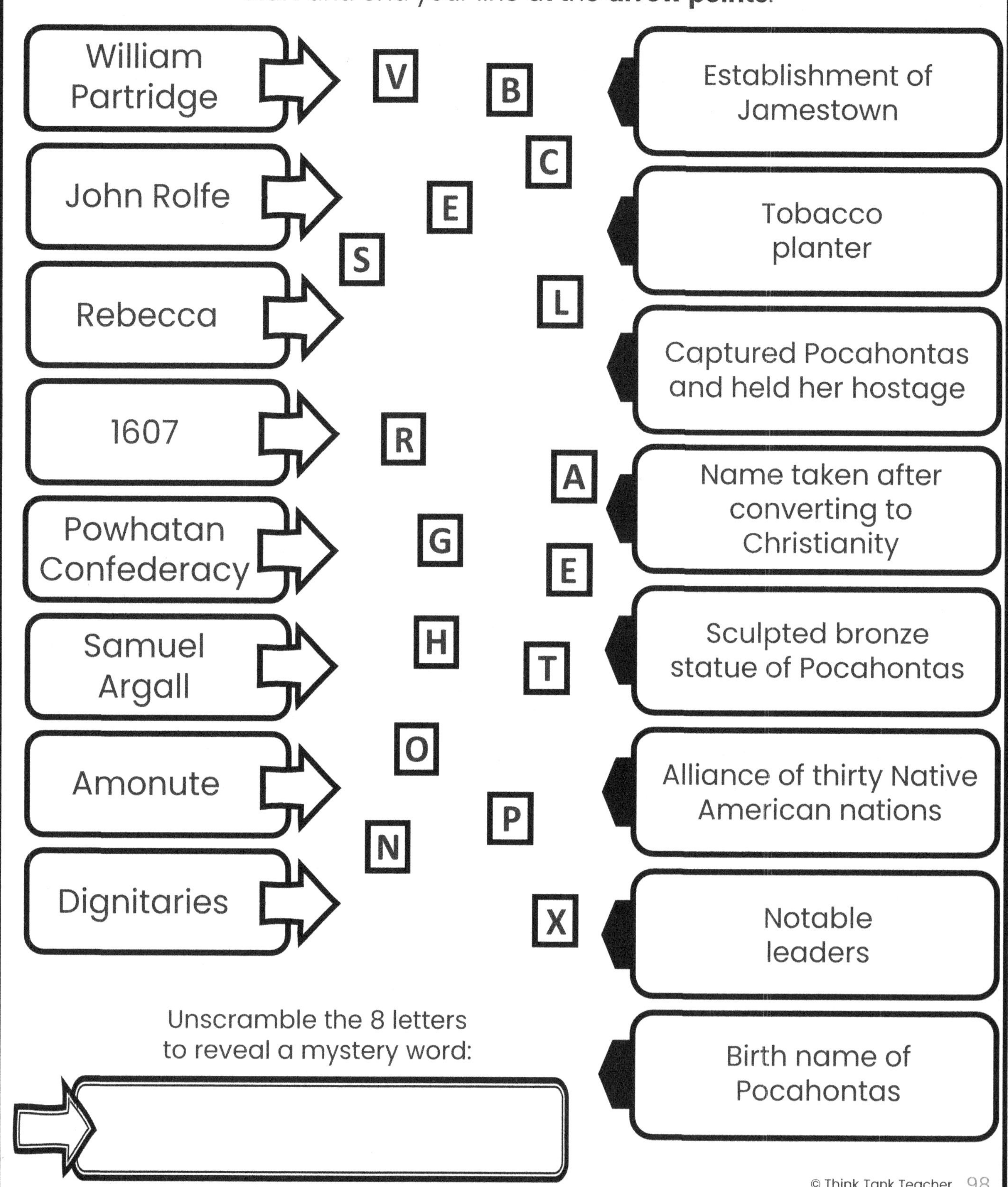

William Partridge
John Rolfe
Rebecca
1607
Powhatan Confederacy
Samuel Argall
Amonute
Dignitaries
V
B
C
E
S
L
R
A
G
E
H
T
O
P
N
X
Establishment of Jamestown
Tobacco planter
Captured Pocahontas and held her hostage
Name taken after converting to Christianity
Sculpted bronze statue of Pocahontas
Alliance of thirty Native American nations
Notable leaders
Birth name of Pocahontas

Unscramble the 8 letters to reveal a mystery word:

MULTIPLE CHOICE

After reading about **Pocahontas**, answer each multiple-choice question below. Then, count the number of times you used each letter as an answer (ABCD) to reveal a 4-digit code. Letters may be used more than once or not at all. If a letter option is not used, put a zero in that box.

1 Who was instrumental in the development of tobacco as a cash crop in Virginia?

A. John Smith
B. John Rolfe
C. James Whitmore
D. Henry Rolfe

2 How long did the "Peace of Pocahontas" last?

A. 2 years
B. 8 years
C. 12 years
D. Over 15 years

3 What was the meaning of the nickname "Pocahontas"?

A. Princess warrior
B. Young girl
C. Little mischief
D. Adventurous

4 Who led the establishment of Jamestown?

A. John Smith
B. John Rolfe
C. James Whitmore
D. Henry Rolfe

5 How old was Pocahontas when settlers arrived in Jamestown?

A. Around 5 years old
B. Around 10 years old
C. Around 15 years old
D. Around 20 years old

6 Who taught Pocahontas about Christianity?

A. Reverend Alexander Whitaker
B. Reverend Henry Rolfe
C. Reverend William Partridge
D. Reverend Lewis Stukely

7 Who was Thomas Rolfe left under the care of?

A. Lewis Stukely
B. John Smith
C. William Partridge
D. Alexander Whitaker

8 When was Pocahontas captured by Samuel Argall?

A. 1613
B. 1615
C. 1617
D. 1619

Count how many times you used each letter as a correct answer (ABCD) to determine the 4-digit code. Record your answer in the boxes below.

# of A's	# of B's	# of C's	# of D's

ANSWER KEYS	PAGE
13 Colonies	
New England Colonies	102
Middle Colonies	102
Southern Colonies	103
New England Colonies	
Plymouth	103
Massachusetts Bay	104
New Hampshire	104
Connecticut	105
Rhode Island	105
Salem Witch Trials	106
Middle Colonies	
New York	106
New Jersey	107
Pennsylvania	107
Delaware	108
Southern Colonies	
Virginia	108
Maryland	109
North Carolina	109
South Carolina	110
Georgia	110
Jamestown	111
Roanoke	111
Pocahontas	112

NEW ENGLAND COLONIES

TRUE OR FALSE

After reading about the **New England Colonies**, read each statement below and determine if it is true or false. If the statement is true, color the coin that corresponds with that question. If the statement is false, cross out that coin value. When you are finished, add the TOTAL of **ALL TRUE** coin values to reveal a 4-digit code. One digit of the code has been provided for you. If the total is 625, a 6 would go in the first box, the 2 in the second box and so on.

A. The English often imposed their laws and practices on the Native Americans.

B. In the 1600s, England was experiencing religious turmoil (chaos).

C. As the governor of Plymouth, John Mason helped the Pilgrims survive their early years in New England.

D. The New England Colonies included Maine, Pennsylvania, Ohio, and Connecticut.

E. Rhode Island was founded by William Bradford.

F. Religion was the cornerstone of life in the New England Colonies.

G. The Pilgrims sought to separate entirely from the Church of England.

H. Rhode Island became a place for Puritans and Quakers to express religious beliefs publicly.

After shading the coins based on your answer, add the value of ALL TRUE statements to get the final total. Record your answer in the boxes below.

2	5	0	7

DOUBLE PUZZLE

After reading about the **New England Colonies**, determine the word that corresponds with the statements provided below. Spell the corresponding word in the boxes to the right. You may or may not use all squares provided for each answer. Any numerical answers must be spelled out. Next, use the numbers **under** indicated letters to reveal a secret word.

#	Statement	Answer	Number under letter
1	Last name of the founder of Connecticut	H O O K E R	2 (under E)
2	Wampanoag chief during King Philip's War	M E T A C O M	
3	Last name of the founder of Rhode Island	W I L L I A M S	4 (under I)
4	A territory governed and controlled by a distant country	C O L O N Y	
5	Wanted to reform the Church of England	P U R I T A N S	8 (under N)
6	Forced to leave	E X I L E D	6 (under I)
7	Name of the ship the Pilgrims sailed on	M A Y F L O W E R	3 (under L)
8	Last name of the governor of Plymouth	B R A D F O R D	7 (under O)
9	New Hampshire became a ___ province in 1679	R O Y A L	1 (under R)
10	Also known as separatists	P I L G R I M S	5 (under G)

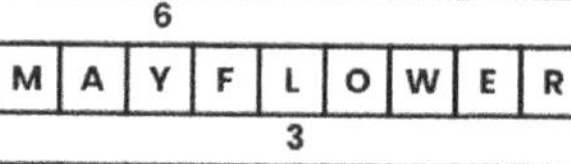

SECRET WORD

R	E	L	I	G	I	O	N
1	2	3	4	5	6	7	8

MIDDLE COLONIES

PARAGRAPH CODE

After reading about the **Middle Colonies**, head back to the reading and number ALL the paragraphs in the reading passage. Then, read each statement below and determine which paragraph **NUMBER** the statement can be found in. Paragraph numbers MAY be used more than one time or not at all. Follow the directions below to reveal the 4-digit code.

	Statement	Paragraph
A	The first permanent European settlement in Delaware was named Fort Christina, and the region became known as New Sweden.	6
B	Edward Hyde was appointed (chosen) the first governor of the royal colony.	4
C	These ports facilitated trade not only between the colonies but also with Europe, Africa, and the Caribbean.	9
D	They offered a mix of agriculture, industry, and trade that set them apart from both the New England and Southern colonies.	1
E	In 1609, Henry Hudson navigated up the Hudson River to Albany, New York, and explored the Delaware Bay on behalf of the Dutch East India Company.	2
F	Farmers typically produced enough for their own families while having surplus crops to sell or trade.	8
G	New York was originally settled by the Dutch as New Netherland in 1626.	3
H	William Penn's charter guaranteed freedom of religion, promoted religious tolerance and democratic governance.	5

ELIMINATE ALL EVEN-NUMBERED paragraphs that you used as an answer. Record the remaining numbers (in the SAME order in which you recorded them above) in the boxes below.

9	1	3	5

MYSTERY WORD

After reading about the **Middle Colonies**, determine if each statement below is true or false. Color or shade the boxes of the **TRUE** statements. Next, unscramble the mystery word using the large letters of the **TRUE** statements.

Delaware was founded by Peter Minuit. **R**	Carpenters built homes, barns, bridges, and other infrastructures necessary for daily life. **E**	The first permanent European settlement in Delaware was named Fort Christina. **C**	The counties in Delaware established their own assembly in 1704. **L**
Delaware's rivers provided routes for transporting goods to larger hubs. **T**	In 1609, Francis Drake navigated up the Hudson River to Albany, New York. **S**	In 1681, William Penn, a Quaker, received a land grant from King Charles II. **U**	Queen Anne reunited East and West Jersey in 1702. **I**
Edward Hyde was appointed the first governor of the royal colony of Vermont. **D**	Middle Colonies included New York, Pennsylvania, New Jersey and Delaware. **R**	New York was originally settled by the German. **P**	Traditionally, blacksmiths worked with iron and steel. **U**
King Charles II granted the land to his brother, the Duke of York. **A**	William Penn's charter guaranteed freedom of religion. **G**	Delaware later came under English control in 1687. **B**	The poor soil in the Middle Colonies only supported a small range of crops. **O**

Unscramble the word using the large bold letters of only the **TRUE** statements.

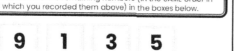

AGRICULTURE

SOUTHERN COLONIES

MYSTERY MATCH

After reading about the **Southern Colonies**, draw a line from the left-hand column to make a match in the right-hand column. Your line should go through **ONE** letter. When you complete all the matches, use the letters with a line THROUGH them to unscramble a mystery word. You MUST start and end your line at the **arrow points**.

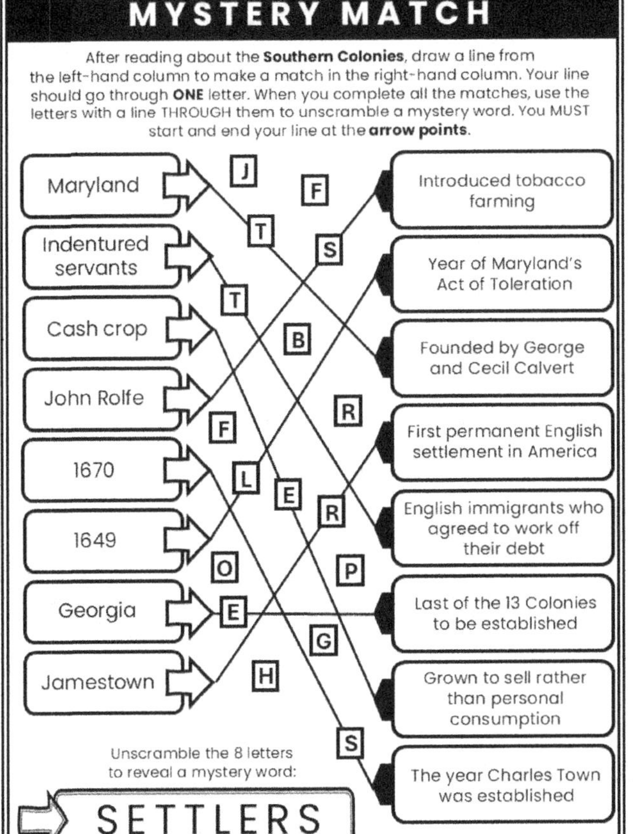

Maryland
Indentured servants
Cash crop
John Rolfe
1670
1649
Georgia
Jamestown
J
F
T
S
T
B
R
F
L
E
R
O
P
E
G
H
S
Introduced tobacco farming
Year of Maryland's Act of Toleration
Founded by George and Cecil Calvert
First permanent English settlement in America
English immigrants who agreed to work off their debt
Last of the 13 Colonies to be established
Grown to sell rather than personal consumption
The year Charles Town was established

Unscramble the 8 letters to reveal a mystery word:

SETTLERS

© Think Tank Teacher

MULTIPLE CHOICE

After reading about the **Southern Colonies**, answer each multiple-choice question below. Then, count the number of times you used each letter as an answer (ABCD) to reveal a 4-digit code. Letters may be used more than once or not at all. If a letter option is not used, put a zero in that box.

1 Which colony was founded by James Oglethorpe?

A. Maryland
B. Georgia
C. South Carolina
D. Virginia

2 Which colony, with extensive pine forests, became a leading producer of tar and turpentine?

A. Maryland
B. Georgia
C. Virginia
D. North Carolina

3 Who granted Carolina to the Lords Proprietors?

A. King George III
B. King James I
C. Queen Victoria
D. King Charles II

4 When was Jamestown established?

A. 1607
B. 1617
C. 1627
D. 1637

5 How long did indentured servants agree to work for to pay off their debt?

A. 1-3 years
B. 4-7 years
C. 8-11 years
D. 12-15 years

6 Who was known as Lord Baltimore?

A. George Calvert
B. John Rolfe
C. James Oglethorpe
D. John Smith

7 What was the transatlantic slave trade also known as?

A. Circular Trade
B. Triangular Trade
C. Linear Trade
D. Indentured Trade

8 Which colony was named after Queen Henrietta Maria?

A. Maryland
B. Georgia
C. Virginia
D. North Carolina

Count how many times you used each letter as a correct answer (ABCD) to determine the 4-digit code. Record your answer in the boxes below.

# of A's	# of B's	# of C's	# of D's
3	3	0	2

© Think Tank Teacher

PLYMOUTH

TRUE OR FALSE

After reading about **Plymouth**, read each statement below and determine if it is true or false. If the statement is true, color the coin that corresponds with that question. If the statement is false, cross out that coin value. When you are finished, add the TOTAL of **ALL TRUE** coin values to reveal a 4-digit code. One digit of the code has been provided for you. If the total is 625, a 6 would go in the first box, the 2 in the second box and so on.

A. In 1621, the Pilgrims had their first harvest.

B. The voyage across the Atlantic Ocean took nine months to reach New England.

C. Due to disease brought by Europeans, entire Wampanoag villages were wiped out.

D. Captain William Bradford was commander of the Mayflower.

E. Many Pilgrims were a part of a religious group called "Separatists."

F. There was a total of one-hundred-two passengers and about thirty crewmen on the Mayflower.

G. There were two ships the Pilgrims set sail on to America: the Nina and the Pinta.

H. Women and children were not allowed to sign the Mayflower Compact.

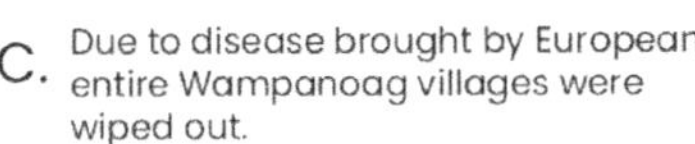

A 75 · E 100 · C 50 · F 75 · H 25

After shading the coins based on your answer, add the value of ALL TRUE statements to get the final total. Record your answer in the boxes below.

3	2	5	3

© Think Tank Teacher

DOUBLE PUZZLE

After reading about **Plymouth**, determine the word that corresponds with the statements provided below. Spell the corresponding word in the boxes to the right. You may or may not use all squares provided for each answer. Any numerical answers must be spelled out. Next, use the numbers **under** indicated letters to reveal a secret word.

#	Clue	Answer	Number under letter
1	The month the Mayflower set sail for America	SEPTEMBER	4 (under P)
2	Original destination of the Mayflower	VIRGINIA	6 (under N)
3	Pilgrims set sail on two ships: the Mayflower and the ___	SPEEDWELL	1 (under W)
4	Last name of governor after John Carver passed away	BRADFORD	8 (under A)
5	Passengers who just wanted a better life	STRANGERS	
6	Taught the pilgrims how to plant corn	SQUANTO	5 (under A)
7	The voyage across the ___ Ocean took two months	ATLANTIC	2 (under A)
8	The Mayflower ___ established legal order	COMPACT	3 (under M)
9	Last name of the Mayflower's captain	JONES	7 (under O)
10	Separatists wanted to separate from the Church of ___	ENGLAND	9 (under G)

SECRET WORD

W	A	M	P	A	N	O	A	G
1	2	3	4	5	6	7	8	9

© Think Tank Teacher

MASSACHUSETTS BAY

PARAGRAPH CODE

After reading about **Massachusetts Bay**, head back to the reading and number ALL the paragraphs in the reading passage. Then, read each statement below and determine which paragraph **NUMBER** the statement can be found in. Paragraph numbers MAY be used more than one time or not at all. Follow the directions below to reveal the 4-digit code.

	Statement	#
A	The Puritan church and the government were closely linked, with only male church members allowed to vote or hold office.	7
B	Williams went on to found Rhode Island, which became known for its greater religious tolerance.	10
C	In this kind of society, what the church said often influenced what happened in the community.	7
D	The settlers engaged in fishing, farming, and shipbuilding.	8
E	The name "Massachusetts" translates to "at the great hill."	4
F	The Massachusetts Bay Colony formed the foundation for much of New England's development.	1
G	The Puritans were a group of Protestant Christians known for their strict religious beliefs and practices.	2
H	The Massachusetts Bay Colony faced various challenges, including internal disputes and conflicts with Native Americans.	9

ELIMINATE ALL EVEN-NUMBERED paragraphs that you used as an answer. Record the remaining numbers (in the SAME order in which you recorded them above) in the boxes below.

7 7 1 9

MYSTERY WORD

After reading about **Massachusetts Bay**, determine if each statement below is true or false. Color or shade the boxes of the **TRUE** statements. Next, unscramble the mystery word using the large letters of the **TRUE** statements.

Winthrop named the colony after the Algonquin. **H**	King Philip's War was fought by Spanish settlers and the French. **A**	The Pequot War took place from 1673-1675. **C**	The colony of Massachusetts Bay benefited from its proximity to the ocean. **R**
Roger Williams went on to found Rhode Island. **I**	Puritans were a strict group of Protestant Christians. **O**	The Massachusetts Bay Company was led by John Rolfe. **U**	Anne Hutchinson was banished in 1702. **L**
Only female church members allowed to vote or hold office. **E**	The Puritans placed a strong emphasis on education. **P**	Puritans of Massachusetts Bay sought to "purify" the Church. **T**	The name "Massachusetts" translates to "the upper house." **K**
Massachusetts Bay Colony was founded in 1607. **D**	Winthrop set sail on the Santa Maria in 1630. **M**	Harvard College was established in 1636. **W**	A dissenter is a person who disagrees with the official beliefs of a particular religion. **N**

Unscramble the word using the large bold letters of only the **TRUE** statements.

NEW HAMPSHIRE

MYSTERY MATCH

After reading about **New Hampshire**, draw a line from the left-hand column to make a match in the right-hand column. Your line should go through **ONE** letter. When you complete all the matches, use the letters with a line THROUGH them to unscramble a mystery word. You MUST start and end your line at the **arrow points**.

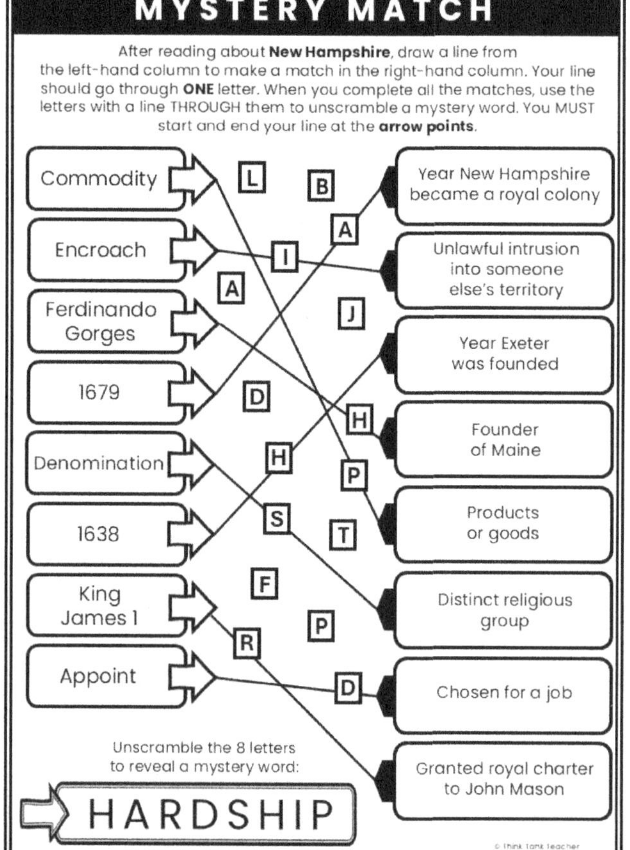

Unscramble the 8 letters to reveal a mystery word:

HARDSHIP

MULTIPLE CHOICE

After reading about **New Hampshire**, answer each multiple-choice question below. Then, count the number of times you used each letter as an answer (ABCD) to reveal a 4-digit code. Letters may be used more than once or not at all. If a letter option is not used, put a zero in that box.

1 What did the economy of New Hampshire rely on?

A. Fishing
B. Timber
C. Agriculture
D. All of the above

2 What did the extensive forests of New Hampshire provide wood for?

A. Construction
B. Fuel
C. Shipbuilding
D. All of the above

3 In the 1600s, when Europeans arrived, who was the New Hampshire region home to?

A. Abenaki
B. Pennacook
C. Algonquian
D. All of the above

4 Mason was the former governor of what region?

A. Providence
B. Exeter
C. Newfoundland
D. Jamestown

5 Mason and Gorges split the land based on what river?

A. Punxatawny River
B. Piscataqua River
C. Potomac River
D. None of the above

6 What religious groups settled in New Hampshire?

A. Quakers
B. Anglicans
C. Puritans
D. All of the above

7 When was Captain Mason granted a royal charter by King James I?

A. 1609
B. 1619
C. 1629
D. 1639

8 Who founded Exeter, New Hampshire?

A. Wheelwright
B. Gorges
C. Jones
D. Williams

Count how many times you used each letter as a correct answer (ABCD) to determine the 4-digit code. Record your answer in the boxes below.

# of A's	# of B's	# of C's	# of D's
1	1	2	4

CONNECTICUT

TRUE OR FALSE

After reading about **Connecticut**, read each statement below and determine if it is true or false. If the statement is true, color the coin that corresponds with that question. If the statement is false, cross out that coin value. When you are finished, add the TOTAL of **ALL TRUE** coin values to reveal a 4-digit code. One digit of the code has been provided for you. If the total is 625, a 6 would go in the first box, the 2 in the second box and so on.

A 75

A. In 1662, the Connecticut Colony received a Royal Charter from the King of England.

B. Under the newly established constitution, John Haynes was chosen as the governor.

C. The Fundamental Orders of Connecticut was adopted in 1687.

D. Puritan beliefs emphasized hard work, community, and a strict moral code.

E. Dutch privateer John Winthrop was the first European to explore Connecticut in 1602.

F. The Fundamental Orders required colonists to be members of the Puritan church in order to vote.

G. The Connecticut Colony was founded in 1636 by Thomas Hooker.

H. "Quinnehtukqut" means "land on the long tidal river."

B 25

G 50

D 100

H 25

After shading the coins based on your answer, add the value of ALL TRUE statements to get the final total. Record your answer in the boxes below.

2	7	5	0

DOUBLE PUZZLE

After reading about **Connecticut**, determine the word that corresponds with the statements provided below. Spell the corresponding word in the boxes to the right. You may or may not use all squares provided for each answer. Any numerical answers must be spelled out. Next, use the numbers **under** indicated letters to reveal a secret word.

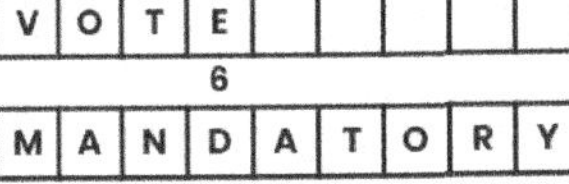

1	Hooker believed all Christians should have the right to ___	V O T E (6 under E)
2	Attendance at church services was ___	M A N D A T O R Y
3	Pequot chief	T A T O B E M
4	John Haynes was chosen as the ___	G O V E R N O R (2 under N)
5	"Quinnehtukqut" means "land on the long ___ river"	T I D A L (3 under I)
6	___ provided oil, which was used for lamps	W H A L I N G (5 under I)
7	The Fundamental ___ of Connecticut was adopted in 1639	O R D E R S (7 under D)
8	Last name of the only trained lawyer in Connecticut	L U D L O W (1 under U)
9	Last name of the first Dutch privateer to explore Connecticut	B L O C K
10	Hooker's group settled in what would become ___	H A R T F O R D (4 under F)

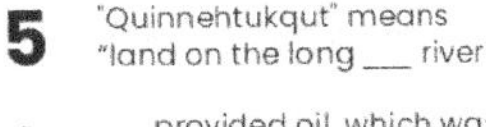
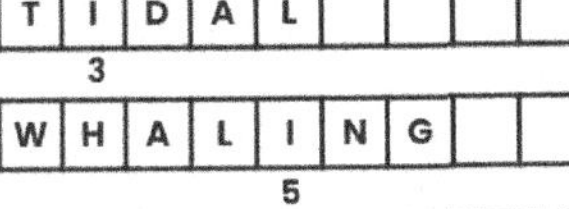
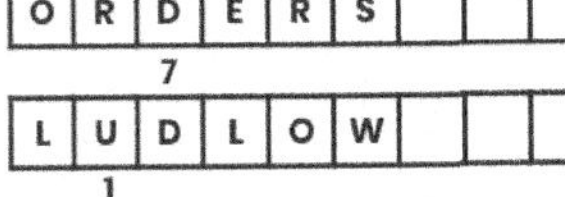
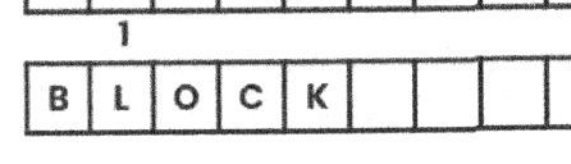

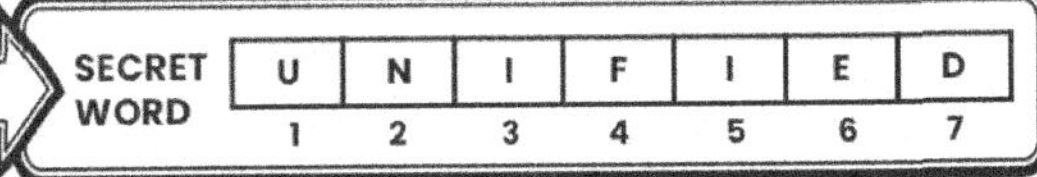

SECRET WORD

U	N	I	F	I	E	D
1	2	3	4	5	6	7

RHODE ISLAND

PARAGRAPH CODE

After reading about **Rhode Island**, head back to the reading and number ALL the paragraphs in the reading passage. Then, read each statement below and determine which paragraph **NUMBER** the statement can be found in. Paragraph numbers MAY be used more than one time or not at all. Follow the directions below to reveal the 4-digit code.

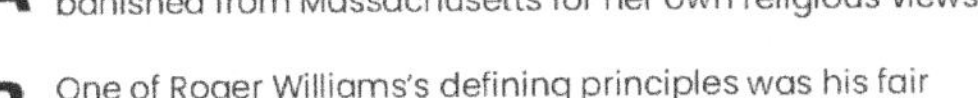

	Statement	#
A	Anne Hutchinson founded Portsmouth in 1638 after being banished from Massachusetts for her own religious views.	4
B	One of Roger Williams's defining principles was his fair treatment of Native Americans.	9
C	Rhode Island also played a controversial role in the triangular trade.	6
D	Williams, a religious dissenter, was originally a Puritan minister in the Massachusetts Bay Colony.	2
E	The coastal waters made shipbuilding another key industry in the colony.	5
F	The war resulted in significant destruction in Rhode Island, with Providence itself being burned.	10
G	Settlers farmed crops like corn, wheat, and barley, while raising livestock such as cattle and pigs.	5
H	This made it a safe haven for groups like Quakers, Baptists, Jews, and others who faced persecution elsewhere in New England.	7

ELIMINATE ALL EVEN-NUMBERED paragraphs that you used as an answer. Record the remaining numbers (in the SAME order in which you recorded them above) in the boxes below.

9	5	5	7

MYSTERY WORD

After reading about **Rhode Island**, determine if each statement below is true or false. Color or shade the boxes of the **TRUE** statements. Next, unscramble the mystery word using the large letters of the **TRUE** statements.

Rhode Island allowed people of various beliefs to worship as they chose. **N**	Providence was burned during King Philip's War. **I**	King Philip was also known as Tatobem. **P**	Williams fled north and settled near Chesapeake Bay after being banished. **M**
Narragansett eventually joined King Philip against the English settlers. **T**	In 1663, the colony was granted a new charter by King Charles II of England. **S**	Williams purchased land from the Narragansett. **S**	Rhode Island was founded by Roger Williams in 1636. **E**
Williams was originally a Puritan minister in the Georgia Colony. **J**	King Philip's War took place from 1775-1776. **F**	To be banished means forced to leave. **S**	Early on, the colony's economy centered on farming, fishing, and trade. **E**
Coddington and Clarke went on to found the settlement of Newport in 1639. **D**	Roger Williams believed that religion should be a personal matter. **R**	Anne Hutchinson founded Warwick in 1632. **B**	Rhode Island was established in the late 15th century. **C**

Unscramble the word using the large bold letters of only the **TRUE** statements.

DISSENTERS

SALEM WITCH TRIALS

MYSTERY MATCH

After reading about the **Salem Witch Trials**, draw a line from the left-hand column to make a match in the right-hand column. Your line should go through **ONE** letter. When you complete all the matches, use the letters with a line THROUGH them to unscramble a mystery word. You MUST start and end your line at the **arrow points**.

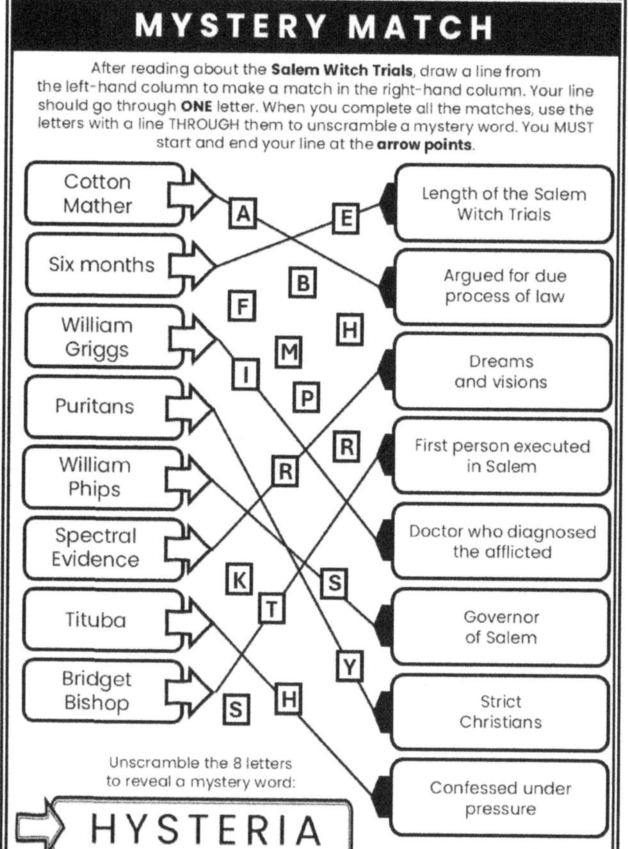

Unscramble the 8 letters to reveal a mystery word:

HYSTERIA

MULTIPLE CHOICE

After reading about the **Salem Witch Trials**, answer each multiple-choice question below. Then, count the number of times you used each letter as an answer (ABCD) to reveal a 4-digit code. Letters may be used more than once or not at all. If a letter option is not used, put a zero in that box.

1 What were the special witchcraft courts known as?

A. Court of Common Pleas
B. Court of Exchequer
C. Court of Oyer and Terminer
D. None of the above

2 When were the last of the witchcraft trials held?

A. May of 1693
B. June of 1691
C. May of 1697
D. June of 1672

3 In what household did the hysteria of witchcraft begin?

A. Griggs household
B. Mather household
C. Osborn household
D. Parris household

4 Who spoke against convicting women on 'spectral evidence'?

A. Pastor Parris
B. Sarah Osborn
C. Reverend Mather
D. William Griggs

5 What did the afflicted girls do?

A. Twitch
B. Twist their bodies
C. Make strange noises
D. All of the above

6 When did an English law officially declare witchcraft as a capital crime?

A. 1641
B. 1651
C. 1661
D. 1671

7 Who was a homeless beggar arrested for witchcraft?

A. Sarah Good
B. Tituba
C. Sarah Osborn
D. Cotton Mather

8 Once pardoned from jail, how much was each victim paid?

A. Six-hundred British Pounds
B. Twelve-hundred Pesos
C. Fourteen-hundred British Pounds
D. Twenty-four-hundred Pesos

Count how many times you used each letter as a correct answer (ABCD) to determine the 4-digit code. Record your answer in the boxes below.

# of A's	# of B's	# of C's	# of D's
4	0	2	2

NEW YORK

TRUE OR FALSE

After reading about **New York**, read each statement below and determine if it is true or false. If the statement is true, color the coin that corresponds with that question. If the statement is false, cross out that coin value. When you are finished, add the TOTAL of **ALL TRUE** coin values to reveal a 4-digit code. One digit of the code has been provided for you. If the total is 625, a 6 would go in the first box, the 2 in the second box and so on.

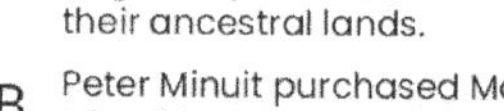
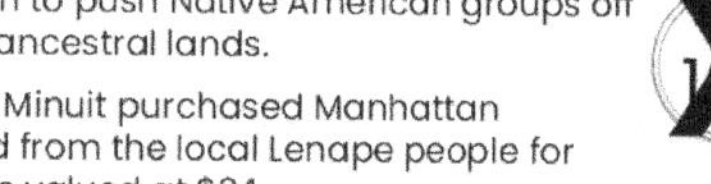
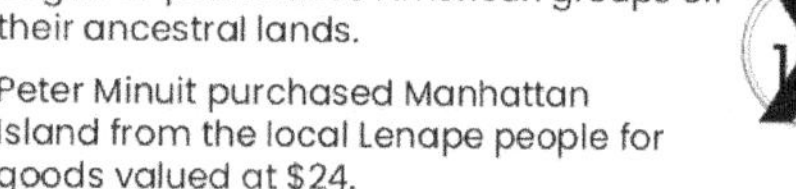

A 75

A. As the English expanded their control, they began to push Native American groups off their ancestral lands.

B. Peter Minuit purchased Manhattan Island from the local Lenape people for goods valued at $24.

B 25

C. Henry Hudson went on to become the first governor of New York.

D. Hudson's ship was called the "Pinta" or New Surface.

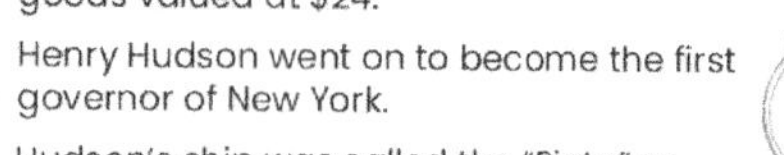

E. The New York Colony was initially founded as New Nassau by the French.

F. New York quickly grew into one of the most prosperous colonies due to its strategic location along the Pacific coast.

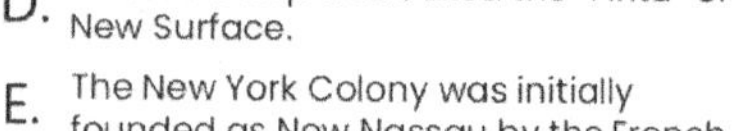

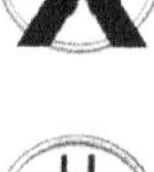

G. In 1614, Fort Bronx became the first Dutch settlement in North America.

H. Most European explorers of the New Land were looking for the legendary Northwest Passage.

H 25

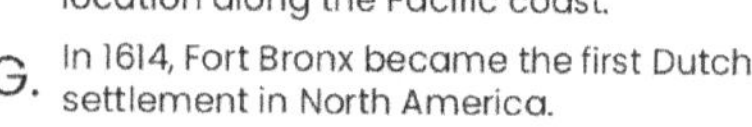
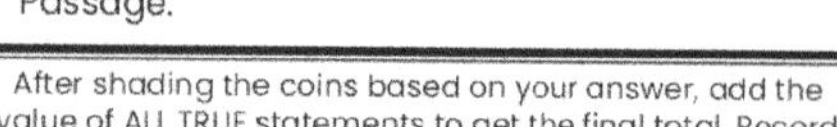

After shading the coins based on your answer, add the value of ALL TRUE statements to get the final total. Record your answer in the boxes below.

1	2	5	9

DOUBLE PUZZLE

After reading about **New York**, determine the word that corresponds with the statements provided below. Spell the corresponding word in the boxes to the right. You may or may not use all squares provided for each answer. Any numerical answers must be spelled out. Next, use the numbers **under** indicated letters to reveal a secret word.

1 New ___ is now present-day New York City — AMSTERDAM

2 Last name of New Netherland's person that purchased Manhattan Island — MINUIT (3 under N)

3 Synonym for forestry — TIMBER

4 The legendary ___ Passage was a water route to Asia — NORTHWEST (4 under O)

5 First name of the Duke of York — JAMES (1 under M)

6 Fort Nassau is now this present-day city in New York — ALBANY (7 under L, 8 under Y)

7 Wealthy investors who received large pieces of land if they brought fifty settlers — PATROONS (6 under O)

8 The Iroquois formed a group called the Five ___ — NATIONS (2 under O)

9 First name of Dutch Governor Stuyvesant — PETER (5 under P)

10 Dutch West ___ Company — INDIA

SECRET WORD

M	O	N	O	P	O	L	Y
1	2	3	4	5	6	7	8

NEW JERSEY

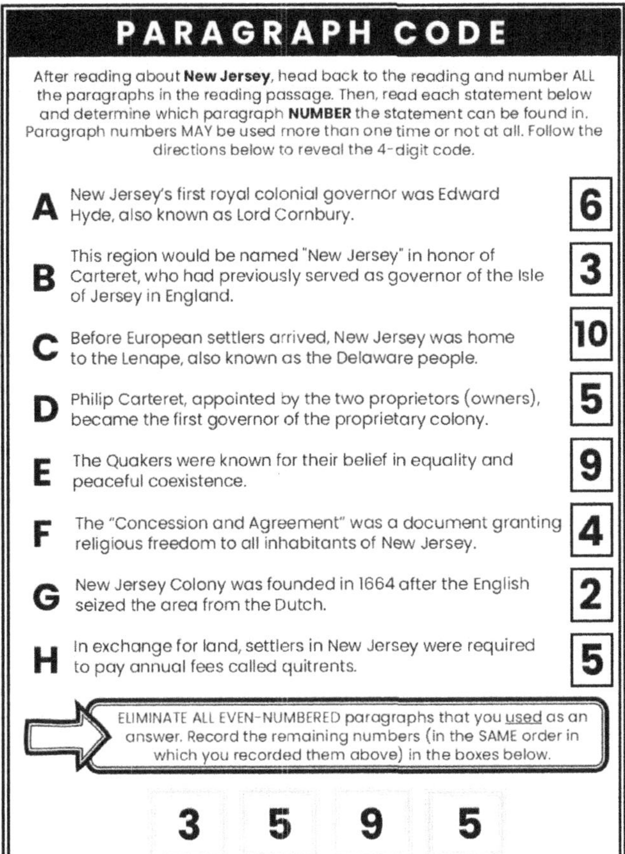

PARAGRAPH CODE

After reading about **New Jersey**, head back to the reading and number ALL the paragraphs in the reading passage. Then, read each statement below and determine which paragraph **NUMBER** the statement can be found in. Paragraph numbers MAY be used more than one time or not at all. Follow the directions below to reveal the 4-digit code.

	Statement	#
A	New Jersey's first royal colonial governor was Edward Hyde, also known as Lord Cornbury.	6
B	This region would be named "New Jersey" in honor of Carteret, who had previously served as governor of the Isle of Jersey in England.	3
C	Before European settlers arrived, New Jersey was home to the Lenape, also known as the Delaware people.	10
D	Philip Carteret, appointed by the two proprietors (owners), became the first governor of the proprietary colony.	5
E	The Quakers were known for their belief in equality and peaceful coexistence.	9
F	The "Concession and Agreement" was a document granting religious freedom to all inhabitants of New Jersey.	4
G	New Jersey Colony was founded in 1664 after the English seized the area from the Dutch.	2
H	In exchange for land, settlers in New Jersey were required to pay annual fees called quitrents.	5

ELIMINATE ALL EVEN-NUMBERED paragraphs that you used as an answer. Record the remaining numbers (in the SAME order in which you recorded them above) in the boxes below.

3 5 9 5

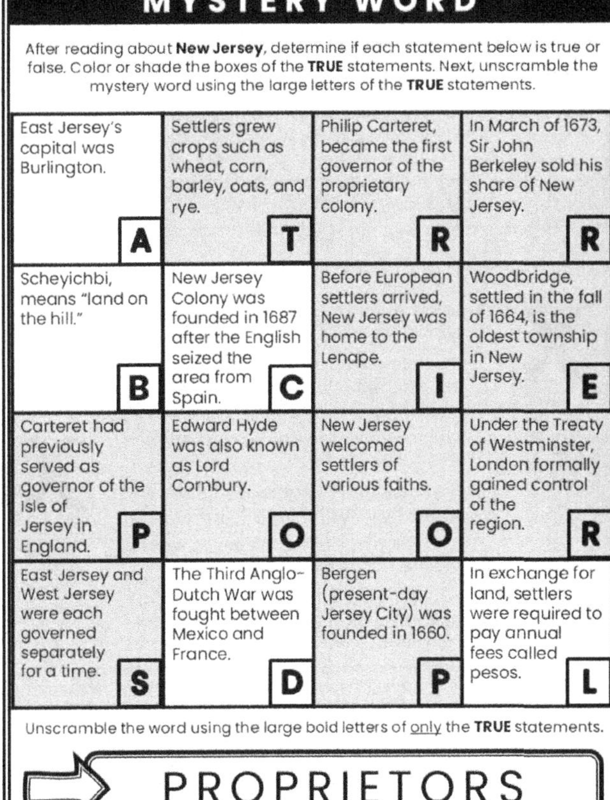

MYSTERY WORD

After reading about **New Jersey**, determine if each statement below is true or false. Color or shade the boxes of the **TRUE** statements. Next, unscramble the mystery word using the large letters of the **TRUE** statements.

East Jersey's capital was Burlington. **A**	Settlers grew crops such as wheat, corn, barley, oats, and rye. **T**	Philip Carteret, became the first governor of the proprietary colony. **R**	In March of 1673, Sir John Berkeley sold his share of New Jersey. **R**
Scheyichbi, means "land on the hill." **B**	New Jersey Colony was founded in 1687 after the English seized the area from Spain. **C**	Before European settlers arrived, New Jersey was home to the Lenape. **I**	Woodbridge, settled in the fall of 1664, is the oldest township in New Jersey. **E**
Carteret had previously served as governor of the Isle of Jersey in England. **P**	Edward Hyde was also known as Lord Cornbury. **O**	New Jersey welcomed settlers of various faiths. **O**	Under the Treaty of Westminster, London formally gained control of the region. **R**
East Jersey and West Jersey were each governed separately for a time. **S**	The Third Anglo-Dutch War was fought between Mexico and France. **D**	Bergen (present-day Jersey City) was founded in 1660. **P**	In exchange for land, settlers were required to pay annual fees called pesos. **L**

Unscramble the word using the large bold letters of only the **TRUE** statements.

PROPRIETORS

PENNSYLVANIA

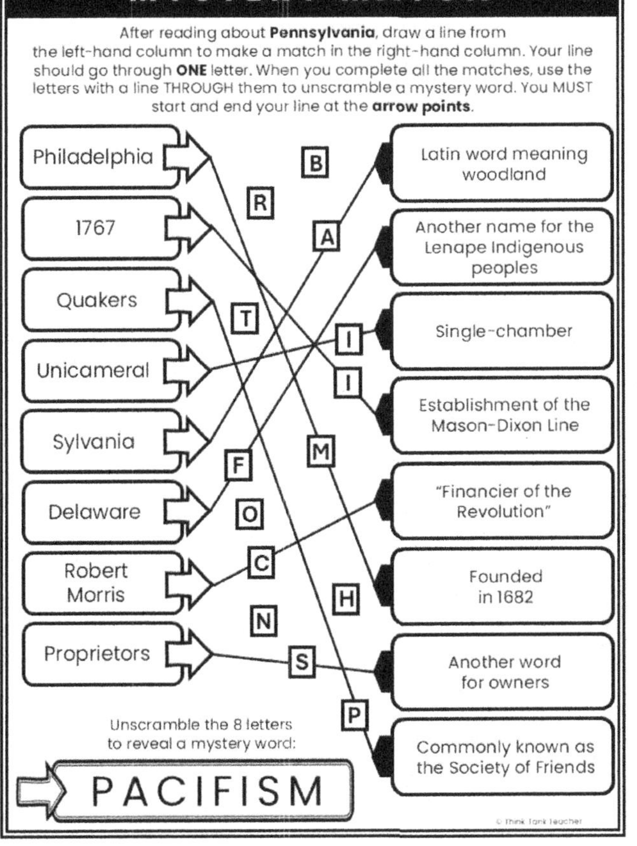

MYSTERY MATCH

After reading about **Pennsylvania**, draw a line from the left-hand column to make a match in the right-hand column. Your line should go through **ONE** letter. When you complete all the matches, use the letters with a line THROUGH them to unscramble a mystery word. You MUST start and end your line at the **arrow points**.

Philadelphia	Latin word meaning woodland
1767	Another name for the Lenape Indigenous peoples
Quakers	Single-chamber
Unicameral	Establishment of the Mason-Dixon Line
Sylvania	"Financier of the Revolution"
Delaware	Founded in 1682
Robert Morris	Another word for owners
Proprietors	Commonly known as the Society of Friends

B R A T I I M F O C H N S P

Unscramble the 8 letters to reveal a mystery word:

PACIFISM

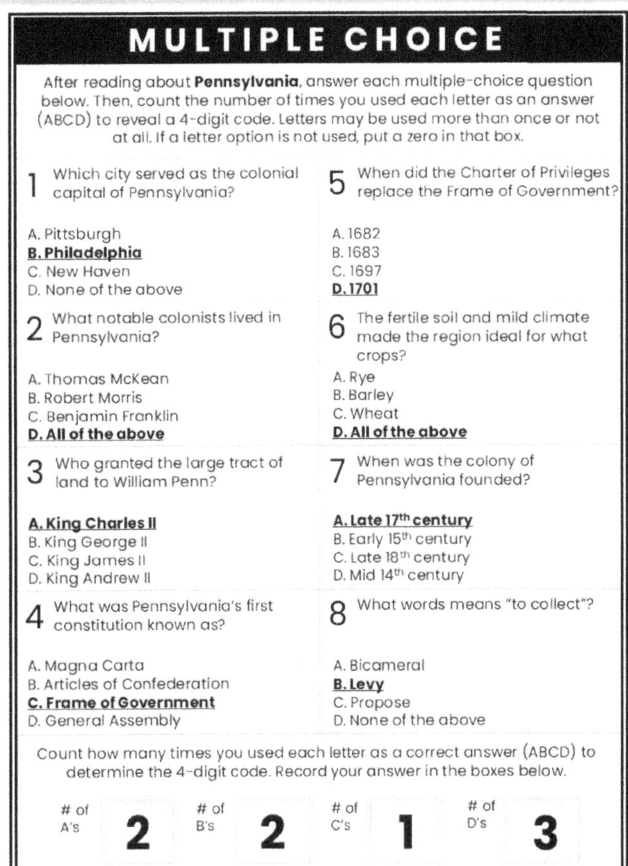

MULTIPLE CHOICE

After reading about **Pennsylvania**, answer each multiple-choice question below. Then, count the number of times you used each letter as an answer (ABCD) to reveal a 4-digit code. Letters may be used more than once or not at all. If a letter option is not used, put a zero in that box.

1 Which city served as the colonial capital of Pennsylvania?

A. Pittsburgh
B. Philadelphia
C. New Haven
D. None of the above

2 What notable colonists lived in Pennsylvania?

A. Thomas McKean
B. Robert Morris
C. Benjamin Franklin
D. All of the above

3 Who granted the large tract of land to William Penn?

A. King Charles II
B. King George II
C. King James II
D. King Andrew II

4 What was Pennsylvania's first constitution known as?

A. Magna Carta
B. Articles of Confederation
C. Frame of Government
D. General Assembly

5 When did the Charter of Privileges replace the Frame of Government?

A. 1682
B. 1683
C. 1697
D. 1701

6 The fertile soil and mild climate made the region ideal for what crops?

A. Rye
B. Barley
C. Wheat
D. All of the above

7 When was the colony of Pennsylvania founded?

A. Late 17th century
B. Early 15th century
C. Late 18th century
D. Mid 14th century

8 What words means "to collect"?

A. Bicameral
B. Levy
C. Propose
D. None of the above

Count how many times you used each letter as a correct answer (ABCD) to determine the 4-digit code. Record your answer in the boxes below.

# of A's	# of B's	# of C's	# of D's
2	2	1	3

DELAWARE

TRUE OR FALSE

After reading about **Delaware**, read each statement below and determine if it is true or false. If the statement is true, color the coin that corresponds with that question. If the statement is false, cross out that coin value. When you are finished, add the TOTAL of **ALL TRUE** coin values to reveal a 4-digit code. One digit of the code has been provided for you. If the total is 625, a 6 would go in the first box, the 2 in the second box and so on.

A. In 1682, the Duke of York transferred control of Delaware to William Penn.

B. Delaware remained under Virginia's administration until 1712.

C. European-introduced diseases, such as smallpox and measles, had a devastating impact on Native American populations.

D. The Delaware River and its coastline provided opportunities for fishing and shipping.

E. Charles Calvert was also known as Lord Baltimore.

F. The Three Lower Counties included New Castle, Sussex, and Kent.

G. The region that is now Delaware was first explored in 1609 by Charles Calvert.

H. In 1638, the Swedes established the first successful European settlement in Delaware, called Fort Christina.

A 75 | B X | C 50 | D 100 | E 100 | F 75 | G X | H 25

After shading the coins based on your answer, add the value of ALL TRUE statements to get the final total. Record your answer in the boxes below.

4	2	5	6

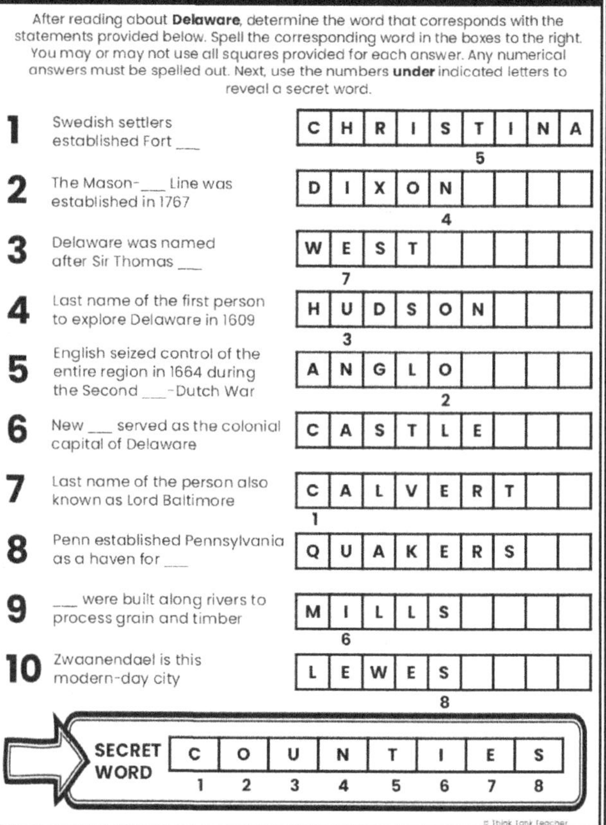

DOUBLE PUZZLE

After reading about **Delaware**, determine the word that corresponds with the statements provided below. Spell the corresponding word in the boxes to the right. You may or may not use all squares provided for each answer. Any numerical answers must be spelled out. Next, use the numbers **under** indicated letters to reveal a secret word.

#	Statement	Answer	Number under letter
1	Swedish settlers established Fort ___	CHRISTINA	5
2	The Mason-___ Line was established in 1767	DIXON	4
3	Delaware was named after Sir Thomas ___	WEST	7
4	Last name of the first person to explore Delaware in 1609	HUDSON	3
5	English seized control of the entire region in 1664 during the Second ___-Dutch War	ANGLO	2
6	New ___ served as the colonial capital of Delaware	CASTLE	
7	Last name of the person also known as Lord Baltimore	CALVERT	1
8	Penn established Pennsylvania as a haven for ___	QUAKERS	
9	___ were built along rivers to process grain and timber	MILLS	6
10	Zwaanendael is this modern-day city	LEWES	8

SECRET WORD

C	O	U	N	T	I	E	S
1	2	3	4	5	6	7	8

VIRGINIA

PARAGRAPH CODE

After reading about **Virginia**, head back to the reading and number ALL the paragraphs in the reading passage. Then, read each statement below and determine which paragraph **NUMBER** the statement can be found in. Paragraph numbers MAY be used more than one time or not at all. Follow the directions below to reveal the 4-digit code.

	Statement	Paragraph
A	The House of Burgesses was made up of twenty-two burgesses, or representatives.	6
B	In 1612, John Rolfe successfully cultivated a strain of tobacco that was highly popular in England.	10
C	This body allowed male property owners to elect representatives who would help make decisions for the colony.	5
D	The Virginia Colony was the first permanent English settlement in North America.	1
E	The church played a significant role in the colony's social and political life, with Anglican ministers often serving as community leaders.	12
F	The company sent three ships - Susan Constant, Godspeed, and Discovery - to the New World, arriving near Chesapeake Bay.	2
G	Subsistence farming is when farmers grow crops and raise livestock mainly to feed themselves and their families.	9
H	The economy of the Virginia Colony was initially based on subsistence farming, fishing, and trading with Native Americans.	9

ELIMINATE ALL EVEN-NUMBERED paragraphs that you used as an answer. Record the remaining numbers (in the SAME order in which you recorded them above) in the boxes below.

5	1	9	9

MYSTERY WORD

After reading about **Virginia**, determine if each statement below is true or false. Color or shade the boxes of the **TRUE** statements. Next, unscramble the mystery word using the large letters of the **TRUE** statements.

In 1624, King James I revoked (canceled) the Virginia Company's charter. **L**	In 1775, the burgesses listened to Patrick Henry deliver his famous speech. **A**	The Anglican Church was also known as the Church of England. **S**	In 1597, Sir Thomas Dale arrived in Virginia with nine-hundred new settlers. **N**
The three ships sent to Virginia were the Nina, Pinta, and Santa Maria. **G**	The Virginia Colony was the first permanent English settlement in North America. **B**	Jamestown faced significant challenges in its early years. **Y**	In 1632, the House of Burgesses was established. **O**
Jefferson served in the House of Burgesses from 1769-1775. **S**	The House of Burgesses was made up of thirty-one burgesses. **C**	Cash crops were grown specifically to sell. **M**	In 1618, John Smith successfully cultivated a strain of tobacco. **R**
Jamestown was established along the Mississippi River. **H**	The Powhatan Confederacy was a network of Algonquian-speaking groups. **E**	George Washington served in the House of Burgesses for 27 years. **P**	The Virginia Company of London was established by King George III. **K**

Unscramble the word using the large bold letters of only the **TRUE** statements.

ASSEMBLY

MARYLAND

MYSTERY MATCH

After reading about **Maryland**, draw a line from the left-hand column to make a match in the right-hand column. Your line should go through **ONE** letter. When you complete all the matches, use the letters with a line THROUGH them to unscramble a mystery word. You MUST start and end your line at the **arrow points**.

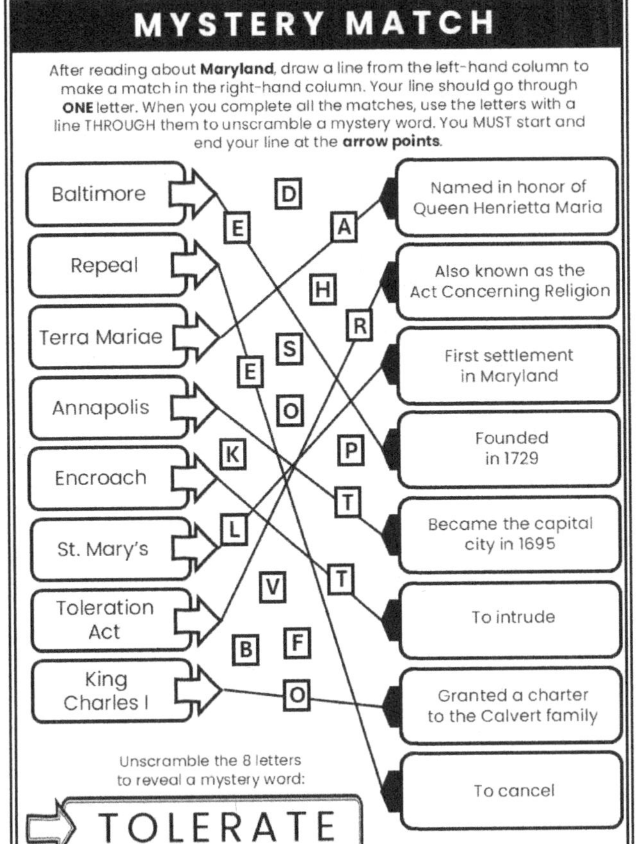

Unscramble the 8 letters to reveal a mystery word:

TOLERATE

© Think Tank Teacher

MULTIPLE CHOICE

After reading about **Maryland**, answer each multiple-choice question below. Then, count the number of times you used each letter as an answer (ABCD) to reveal a 4-digit code. Letters may be used more than once or not at all. If a letter option is not used, put a zero in that box.

1 When was the Maryland Toleration Act passed?

A. 1649
B. 1659
C. 1629
D. 1639

2 When European settlers arrived in Maryland, who did they encounter?

A. Piscataway
B. Algonquian-speaking groups
C. Susquehannock
D. All of the above

3 What bay was Maryland located along?

A. Bay of Bengal
B. Chesapeake Bay
C. Apalachee Bay
D. Galveston Bay

4 Who was the wife of King Charles I?

A. Queen Victoria Marie
B. Queen Henrietta Maria
C. Queen Elizabeth III
D. None of the above

5 What challenges did Maryland face in its early years?

A. Disputes with neighboring colonies
B. Internal religious conflicts
C. Economic struggles
D. All of the above

6 What two ships arrived in Maryland in 1634?

A. Discovery and Susan Constant
B. Ark and Dove
C. Mayflower and Speedwell
D. Nina and Pinta

7 Who was known as the first Lord Baltimore?

A. Cecil Calvert
B. George Calvert
C. Leonard Calvert
D. Michael Calvert

8 What does legislate mean?

A. Remove from office
B. Pass a law
C. Intrusion
D. None of the above

Count how many times you used each letter as a correct answer (ABCD) to determine the 4-digit code. Record your answer in the boxes below.

# of A's	# of B's	# of C's	# of D's
1	5	0	2

© Think Tank Teacher

NORTH CAROLINA

TRUE OR FALSE

After reading about **North Carolina**, read each statement below and determine if it is true or false. If the statement is true, color the coin that corresponds with that question. If the statement is false, cross out that coin value. When you are finished, add the TOTAL of **ALL TRUE** coin values to reveal a 4-digit code. One digit of the code has been provided for you. If the total is 625, a 6 would go in the first box, the 2 in the second box and so on.

A. By 1738, about half the Catawba were wiped out by a smallpox epidemic.

B. In 1705, the first permanent town was established in Bath, North Carolina.

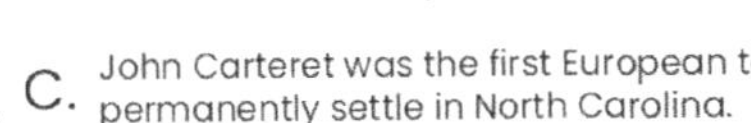

C. John Carteret was the first European to permanently settle in North Carolina.

D. North Carolina became known for its small family farms rather than vast plantations.

E. Carolina comes from the Latin word "Carolus," which means cattle.

F. The Cape Fear settlement was abandoned in 1667.

G. King Charles II of England granted a large charter to eight Lord Proprietors.

H. Sir Walter Raleigh attempted to establish a colony at Roanoke Island.

Coins: A 75, B 25, C ~~100~~, D 100, E ~~50~~, F 75, G 50, H 25

After shading the coins based on your answer, add the value of ALL TRUE statements to get the final total. Record your answer in the boxes below.

3	5	0	3

© Think Tank Teacher

DOUBLE PUZZLE

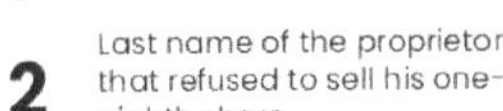

After reading about **North Carolina**, determine the word that corresponds with the statements provided below. Spell the corresponding word in the boxes to the right. You may or may not use all squares provided for each answer. Any numerical answers must be spelled out. Next, use the numbers **under** indicated letters to reveal a secret word.

#	Clue	Answer	Numbered letters
1	First permanent town established in North Carolina	BATH	
2	Last name of the proprietor that refused to sell his one-eighth share	CARTERET	3 (under R)
3	The Tuscarora migrated northward to join the ___ Confederacy	IROQUOIS	
4	The ___ Church became the official church in the 1700s	ANGLICAN	5 (under G)
5	Quakers mostly settled in the ___ region	ALBEMARLE	7 (under L)
6	Synonym for proprietors	OWNERS	1 (under S)
7	Number of proprietors that King Charles I granted charters to	EIGHT	8 (under E), 2 (under T)
8	Carolina comes from the Latin word "___"	CAROLUS	4 (under U)
9	Last name of English explorer that attempted to establish Roanoke	RALEIGH	6 (under G)
10	The Catawba were wiped out by a ___ epidemic	SMALLPOX	9 (under S)

SECRET WORD

S	T	R	U	G	G	L	E	S
1	2	3	4	5	6	7	8	9

© Think Tank Teacher

SOUTH CAROLINA

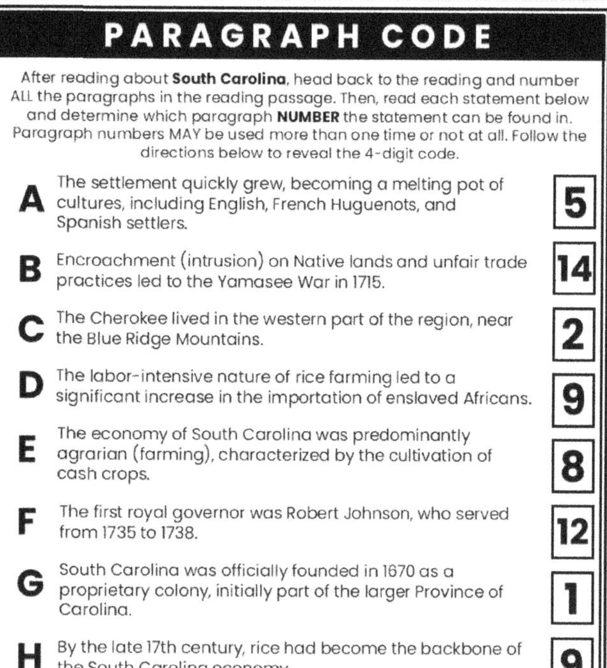

PARAGRAPH CODE

After reading about **South Carolina**, head back to the reading and number ALL the paragraphs in the reading passage. Then, read each statement below and determine which paragraph **NUMBER** the statement can be found in. Paragraph numbers MAY be used more than one time or not at all. Follow the directions below to reveal the 4-digit code.

	Statement	#
A	The settlement quickly grew, becoming a melting pot of cultures, including English, French Huguenots, and Spanish settlers.	5
B	Encroachment (intrusion) on Native lands and unfair trade practices led to the Yamasee War in 1715.	14
C	The Cherokee lived in the western part of the region, near the Blue Ridge Mountains.	2
D	The labor-intensive nature of rice farming led to a significant increase in the importation of enslaved Africans.	9
E	The economy of South Carolina was predominantly agrarian (farming), characterized by the cultivation of cash crops.	8
F	The first royal governor was Robert Johnson, who served from 1735 to 1738.	12
G	South Carolina was officially founded in 1670 as a proprietary colony, initially part of the larger Province of Carolina.	1
H	By the late 17th century, rice had become the backbone of the South Carolina economy.	9

ELIMINATE ALL EVEN-NUMBERED paragraphs that you used as an answer. Record the remaining numbers (in the SAME order in which you recorded them above) in the boxes below.

5 9 1 9

© Think Tank Teacher

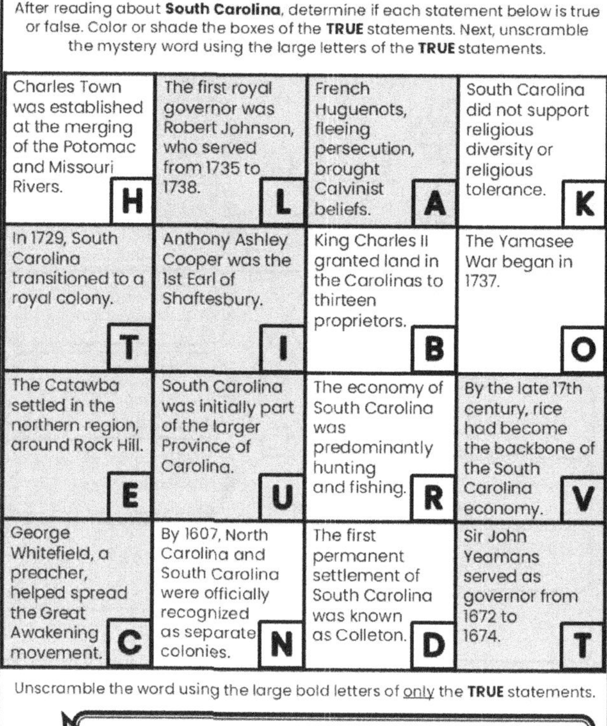

MYSTERY WORD

After reading about **South Carolina**, determine if each statement below is true or false. Color or shade the boxes of the **TRUE** statements. Next, unscramble the mystery word using the large letters of the **TRUE** statements.

Charles Town was established at the merging of the Potomac and Missouri Rivers. **H**	The first royal governor was Robert Johnson, who served from 1735 to 1738. **L**	French Huguenots, fleeing persecution, brought Calvinist beliefs. **A**	South Carolina did not support religious diversity or religious tolerance. **K**
In 1729, South Carolina transitioned to a royal colony. **T**	Anthony Ashley Cooper was the 1st Earl of Shaftesbury. **I**	King Charles II granted land in the Carolinas to thirteen proprietors. **B**	The Yamasee War began in 1737. **O**
The Catawba settled in the northern region, around Rock Hill. **E**	South Carolina was initially part of the larger Province of Carolina. **U**	The economy of South Carolina was predominantly hunting and fishing. **R**	By the late 17th century, rice had become the backbone of the South Carolina economy. **V**
George Whitefield, a preacher, helped spread the Great Awakening movement. **C**	By 1607, North Carolina and South Carolina were officially recognized as separate colonies. **N**	The first permanent settlement of South Carolina was known as Colleton. **D**	Sir John Yeamans served as governor from 1672 to 1674. **T**

Unscramble the word using the large bold letters of only the **TRUE** statements.

CULTIVATE

© Think Tank Teacher

GEORGIA

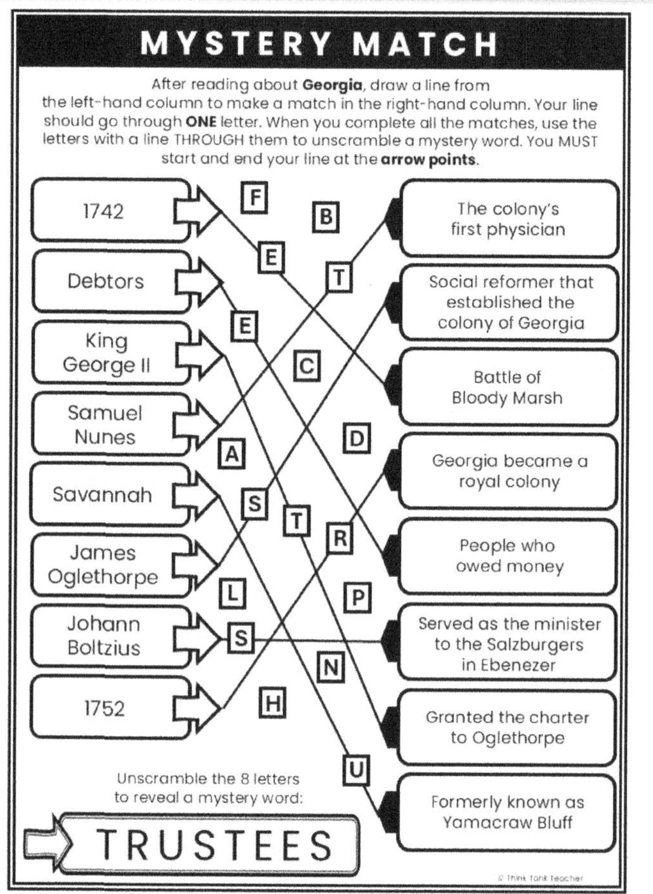

MYSTERY MATCH

After reading about **Georgia**, draw a line from the left-hand column to make a match in the right-hand column. Your line should go through **ONE** letter. When you complete all the matches, use the letters with a line THROUGH them to unscramble a mystery word. You MUST start and end your line at the **arrow points**.

Unscramble the 8 letters to reveal a mystery word:

TRUSTEES

© Think Tank Teacher

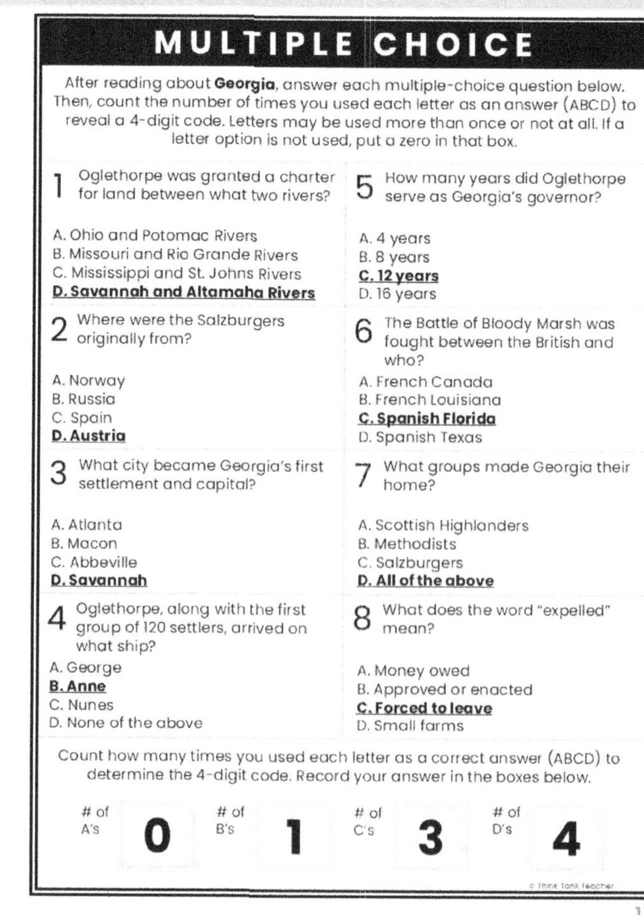

MULTIPLE CHOICE

After reading about **Georgia**, answer each multiple-choice question below. Then, count the number of times you used each letter as an answer (ABCD) to reveal a 4-digit code. Letters may be used more than once or not at all. If a letter option is not used, put a zero in that box.

1 Oglethorpe was granted a charter for land between what two rivers?

A. Ohio and Potomac Rivers
B. Missouri and Rio Grande Rivers
C. Mississippi and St. Johns Rivers
D. Savannah and Altamaha Rivers

2 Where were the Salzburgers originally from?

A. Norway
B. Russia
C. Spain
D. Austria

3 What city became Georgia's first settlement and capital?

A. Atlanta
B. Macon
C. Abbeville
D. Savannah

4 Oglethorpe, along with the first group of 120 settlers, arrived on what ship?

A. George
B. Anne
C. Nunes
D. None of the above

5 How many years did Oglethorpe serve as Georgia's governor?

A. 4 years
B. 8 years
C. 12 years
D. 16 years

6 The Battle of Bloody Marsh was fought between the British and who?

A. French Canada
B. French Louisiana
C. Spanish Florida
D. Spanish Texas

7 What groups made Georgia their home?

A. Scottish Highlanders
B. Methodists
C. Salzburgers
D. All of the above

8 What does the word "expelled" mean?

A. Money owed
B. Approved or enacted
C. Forced to leave
D. Small farms

Count how many times you used each letter as a correct answer (ABCD) to determine the 4-digit code. Record your answer in the boxes below.

# of A's	# of B's	# of C's	# of D's
0	1	3	4

© Think Tank Teacher

JAMESTOWN

TRUE OR FALSE

After reading about **Jamestown**, read each statement below and determine if it is true or false. If the statement is true, color the coin that corresponds with that question. If the statement is false, cross out that coin value. When you are finished, add the TOTAL of **ALL TRUE** coin values to reveal a 4-digit code. One digit of the code has been provided for you. If the total is 625, a 6 would go in the first box, the 2 in the second box and so on.

A 75

A. Jamestown was established in the middle of the Paspahegh territory, a tributary of the Powhatan.

B. In 1616, King George II I revoked the Virginia Company's charter.

C. The colony fell to chaos between 1609 and 1610 when John Smith was injured by a gunpowder explosion.

D. The expedition to the New World included seven hundred twenty-one men.

C 50

G 50

E. The Santa Maria, the smallest ship, was later used in attempts to find the legendary Northwest Passage.

F. Jamestown served as capital of the colony for more than two hundred years.

G. Settlers gave the Powhatan tools, pots, and knives in exchange for food such as corn.

H. The founding of Jamestown in 1617 marked the beginning of the first permanent French settlement in North America.

After shading the coins based on your answer, add the value of ALL TRUE statements to get the final total. Record your answer in the boxes below.

1	7	5	7

DOUBLE PUZZLE

After reading about **Jamestown**, determine the word that corresponds with the statements provided below. Spell the corresponding word in the boxes to the right. You may or may not use all squares provided for each answer. Any numerical answers must be spelled out. Next, use the numbers **under** indicated letters to reveal a secret word.

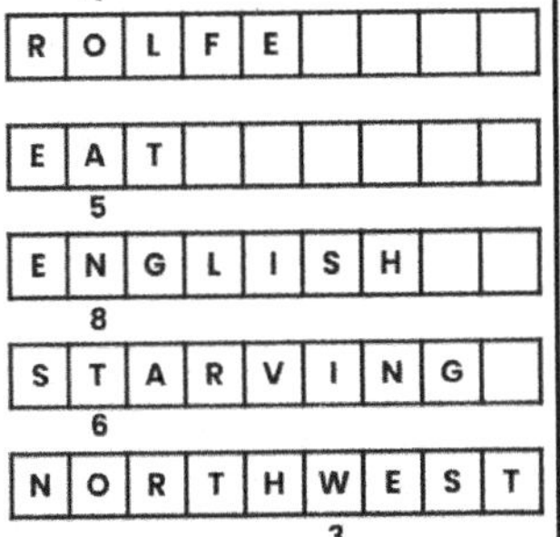

1	Number of ships the group set sail on in December of 1606	T H R E E	4 (under H)
2	Last name of man that introduced tobacco	R O L F E	
3	"If you don't work, you don't ___"	E A T	5 (under A)
4	Jamestown was the first permanent ___ settlement in North America	E N G L I S H	8 (under N)
5	1609-1610 was known as the "___ Time"	S T A R V I N G	6 (under T)
6	The Discovery was used to find the legendary ___ Passage	N O R T H W E S T	3 (under W)
7	The Virginia Company was backed by ___ investors	P R I V A T E	7 (under A)
8	Last name of Jamestown's leader after John Smith	P E R C Y	1 (under P)
9	The Virginia Company of London was a joint-___ company	S T O C K	2 (under O)
10	Colonists selected a location roughly forty miles up this river	J A M E S	

SECRET WORD

P	O	W	H	A	T	A	N
1	2	3	4	5	6	7	8

ROANOKE

PARAGRAPH CODE

After reading about **Roanoke**, head back to the reading and number ALL the paragraphs in the reading passage. Then, read each statement below and determine which paragraph **NUMBER** the statement can be found in. Paragraph numbers MAY be used more than one time or not at all. Follow the directions below to reveal the 4-digit code.

	Statement	Paragraph
A	The disappearance of the Roanoke settlers has sparked numerous theories over the centuries.	12
B	The expedition arrived at Roanoke about one year after Amada and Barlowe looked for places to settle a colony.	4
C	Due to the Spanish Armada, White was not able to return to Roanoke for three years.	9
D	The story of the Lost Colony of Roanoke is one of the oldest mysteries in American history.	1
E	The site of the original Roanoke settlement is now part of the Fort Raleigh National Historic Site.	14
F	There were ninety men, thirteen women, and eleven children.	7
G	England wanted to establish a colony as an attempt to expand the British Empire in the New World.	2
H	Raleigh sent Captain Amada and Captain Barlowe to explore the new area.	3

ELIMINATE ALL EVEN-NUMBERED paragraphs that you used as an answer. Record the remaining numbers (in the SAME order in which you recorded them above) in the boxes below.

9	1	7	3

MYSTERY WORD

After reading about **Roanoke**, determine if each statement below is true or false. Color or shade the boxes of the **TRUE** statements. Next, unscramble the mystery word using the large letters of the **TRUE** statements.

In Roanoke, Greenville left his male settlers under the charge of Ralph Lane. **D**	At the time, England was battling with Spain in the Anglo-Spanish War. **E**	Roanoke was established in the late 19th century. **A**	In 1591, a group of settlers led by John Rolfe arrived at Roanoke. **C**
Sir Richard Greenville led the first expedition to Roanoke Island in 1585. **N**	Roanoke Island is off the coast of present-day Pennsylvania. **L**	Today, the area is called Dare County, North Carolina. **E**	When White returned to Roanoke, he found signs of struggle and stress. **G**
Virginia Dare was the first child born in the Americas to English parents. **C**	Raleigh sent Captain Adrian and Captain Bentley to explore the new area. **H**	Due to the Spanish Armada, White couldn't return to Roanoke for three years. **I**	The supplies to Roanoke arrived as planned, in a timely manner. **R**
Croatoan Island is now known as Cape Canaveral. **T**	Chief Wingina was also known as Squanto. **P**	At Roanoke, Europeans blamed the locals for stealing a silver cup. **E**	In 1584, Queen Elizabeth I granted the land of Virginia to Sir Walter Raleigh. **V**

Unscramble the word using the large bold letters of only the **TRUE** statements.

EVIDENCE

POCAHONTAS

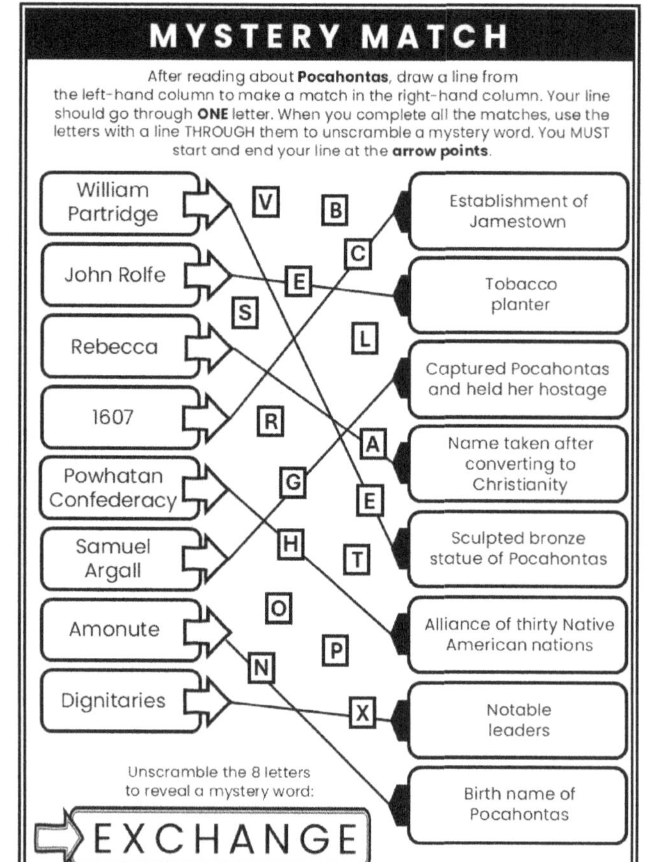

MYSTERY MATCH

After reading about **Pocahontas**, draw a line from the left-hand column to make a match in the right-hand column. Your line should go through **ONE** letter. When you complete all the matches, use the letters with a line THROUGH them to unscramble a mystery word. You MUST start and end your line at the **arrow points**.

Unscramble the 8 letters to reveal a mystery word:

EXCHANGE

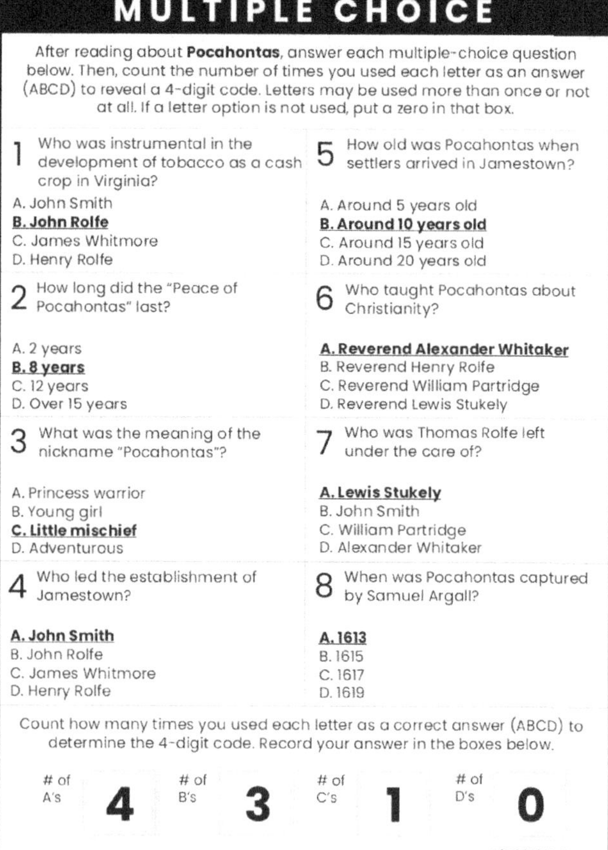

MULTIPLE CHOICE

After reading about **Pocahontas**, answer each multiple-choice question below. Then, count the number of times you used each letter as an answer (ABCD) to reveal a 4-digit code. Letters may be used more than once or not at all. If a letter option is not used, put a zero in that box.

1 Who was instrumental in the development of tobacco as a cash crop in Virginia?

A. John Smith
B. John Rolfe
C. James Whitmore
D. Henry Rolfe

2 How long did the "Peace of Pocahontas" last?

A. 2 years
B. 8 years
C. 12 years
D. Over 15 years

3 What was the meaning of the nickname "Pocahontas"?

A. Princess warrior
B. Young girl
C. Little mischief
D. Adventurous

4 Who led the establishment of Jamestown?

A. John Smith
B. John Rolfe
C. James Whitmore
D. Henry Rolfe

5 How old was Pocahontas when settlers arrived in Jamestown?

A. Around 5 years old
B. Around 10 years old
C. Around 15 years old
D. Around 20 years old

6 Who taught Pocahontas about Christianity?

A. Reverend Alexander Whitaker
B. Reverend Henry Rolfe
C. Reverend William Partridge
D. Reverend Lewis Stukely

7 Who was Thomas Rolfe left under the care of?

A. Lewis Stukely
B. John Smith
C. William Partridge
D. Alexander Whitaker

8 When was Pocahontas captured by Samuel Argall?

A. 1613
B. 1615
C. 1617
D. 1619

Count how many times you used each letter as a correct answer (ABCD) to determine the 4-digit code. Record your answer in the boxes below.

# of A's	# of B's	# of C's	# of D's
4	3	1	0

TERMS OF USE

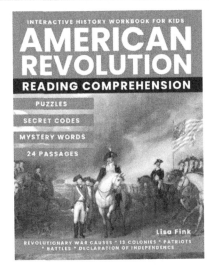

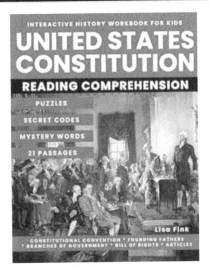

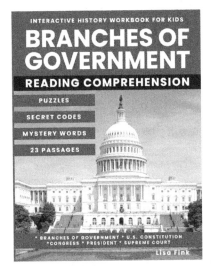

Made in the USA
Columbia, SC
05 December 2024